Before Freud

Before Freud

Neurasthenia and the American Medical Community, 1870–1910

F. G. GOSLING

University of Illinois Press
Urbana and Chicago

This book is printed on acid-free paper.

Library of Congress Cataloging-in-Publication Data

Gosling, Francis G. (Francis George), 1947–
  Before Freud.

  Includes bibliographies and index.
   1. Neurasthenia—Treatment—United States—History—
19th century.   2. Mental illness—Treatment—United
States—History—19th century.   I. Title. [DNLM:
1. Neurasthenia—history—United States. WM 11 AA1 G6b]
RC552.N5G67   1987   616.85′28′060973   87-6038
ISBN 0-252-01406-5

To JR

Contents

Preface

It is common knowledge that in medicine work done only a few years ago is now obsolete. A historical overview of a medical topic can be as enlightening for modern practitioners and researchers, who often know little of their field's past, as it is for the historian trying to understand the relationship between medical practice and the larger society. The perspective gained by looking at developments from a distance in time enables us to draw certain conclusions not only about previous eras but about our own, and may even suggest trends likely to affect the future.

American medical historians have paid particular attention to the late nineteenth century, when discoveries in biology and bacteriology provided the basis for much of what we term modern medicine. While it is a common belief among practitioners that the psychiatric profession is young, dating its modern history from the writings of Sigmund Freud in the early twentieth century, historians have sought the roots of twentieth-century psychiatry in the decades preceding it. Historians such as Gerald Grob and David Rothman have focused on the darker side of psychiatric history—the insane and the politics and philosophy of institutionalization—while others like John and Robin Haller and Anita and Michael Fellman have concentrated on those who promoted mental health, primarily through medical advice literature that counseled Americans on the attainment of health and success through "correct" living.[1] Collectively this literature sheds light on two groups of nineteenth-century Americans—one, the majority of mentally healthy individuals who avidly embraced the values (moderation, rationality, and ambition) of the emerging urban middle class, and the other, a subclass of unfortunates who suffered the torments of insanity. But there was another class of Americans who fell between these extremes, who aspired to a useful place in society but who through some unseen defect of mind or body could not attain mental harmony. These "nervous" Americans and the physicians who treated them are the subjects of this book.

This study makes clear that American physicians in the late nineteenth century recognized neuroses and stress disorders, though in an undifferentiated manner, and believed they could relieve them. The most common diagnosis for such disturbances was neurasthenia, a term that implied weakness of the "nerve force," that mysterious substance that gave vitality to the organism. Scientists believed that they were on the verge of discovering the physiological processes which caused nerve weakness, but in the meantime doctors had to rely on the tools at hand to control or prevent the disease. Therapies therefore included both psychological and physical treatments aimed at conserving and building up the nerve force.

Treatment of neurasthenia varied according to the perceived cause of the illness. Oddly, despite the view that neurasthenia was a single disease, physicians believed that there were several possible causes. Most of these causes were deduced from empirical observation of the patient's lifestyle; a nervous patient was judged to be at fault or blameless for his or her symptoms depending on the doctor's assessment of probable cause. Thus, businessmen were usually found to be suffering from overwork unless they revealed a tendency toward overindulgence in tobacco or alcohol, while laborers were more likely to be suspected of alcohol or drug abuse, exaggerated sexual appetite, or the "secret vice" of masturbation.

Even more pronounced than these class distinctions were the gender differences doctors noted in the causes of neurasthenia. Women were seldom perceived as being overworked, and few were considered guilty of habits of excess. The most likely cause of neurasthenia in women, physicians concluded, was biological. Women were physiologically weaker than men, and the rigors of childbirth, particularly in an age that no longer saw labor and delivery as entirely natural, made them more susceptible to emotional upsets.

These observations helped to put neurasthenia on a scientific footing because they placed the disease in the context of evolutionary ideas. According to the prevailing concepts of nineteenth-century social Darwinism, which applied hereditarian ideas to the study of mankind, the upper classes were more highly evolved than were the lower elements of society and thus had more sensitive nervous systems. Women, having smaller brains, were more emotional than men because they were governed not by their mental processes but by their reproductive systems. Thus neurasthenia achieved popularity partially because it reinforced existing gender and class attitudes; conversely, neurasthenia and its various causes helped to "prove" the validity of dominant social theories.

The study of neurasthenia also reveals many of the social aspects of medical practice in the late nineteenth and early twentieth centuries, as well as the relationship between medical theory and professional practice. Specialism was beginning to emerge as a viable career option, but without the cooperative atmosphere of an established referral system, intense rivalries existed among different types of specialists and between specialists and general practitioners. General practitioners seldom referred mentally distressed patients to specialists; they saw mind and body as inseparable elements of the formula for health. Specialists of various persuasions shared this view and often treated conditions other than those in which they specialized. In terms of Americans' needs for psychological guidance, this meant that help was available much more widely in the late nineteenth and early twentieth centuries than has been supposed (perhaps even more widely than today, given restrictions on insurance coverage for mental conditions). It also meant, on the other hand, that perceived causes and recommended therapies might depend more on the physician's specialty than on the objective symptoms—another observation with contemporary implications.

The increasingly professionalized social and economic environment of late nineteenth-century America witnessed the fragmentation of all fields of expertise, from social work to architecture to engineering. Historians have been particularly interested in the emergence of the middle-class professionals who became the culturally dominant force in the cities created by the new industrial economy.[2] This preoccupation with white-collar professionals has been complemented by studies of those who have ministered to the spiritual and physical needs of the urban middle class.[3] Partially because the well-educated provide historians with more readily available sources, studies of late nineteenth-century American society have tended to focus on cultural elites and have consequently skewed our perception of social reality for many Americans during the period. This tendency has been particularly evident in medical history, where studies have concentrated on major writers and pathbreaking researchers. The implicit assumption of this predominantly hagiographic scholarship is that by analyzing the lives and works of the profession's leaders, we can derive an adequate understanding of the medical reality of the period. In the case of neurasthenia, reliance upon the writings of a small minority of prestigious urban neurologists has created a stereotype of the ailment that is only partially accurate and that obscures the more complex relationship of the disease to the medical community and to American society from 1870 to 1910. While historical information has been gathered on pioneer neurologists like George M. Beard and some of his colleagues in the American Neurological Association (ANA), very little is known about the relatively faceless mass of physicians who also treated neurasthenia. Little has been done to distinguish between the views of the select few and those of the practicing profession who actually treated the majority of neurasthenic sufferers. The question of who treated which patients how, and for what reasons, has not been answered.[4]

Most physicians believed neurasthenia to be especially prevalent among urban middle-class professionals, and neurologists saw such patients with more frequency than lower-class patients. But the reports on neurasthenia from physicians across the country show that the term's diagnostic use extended well beyond prestigious neurologists and their exclusive clientele. Americans of all social classes and a variety of occupations were diagnosed as neurasthenic and treated by rural, urban, and small-town physicians in homes, private offices, public dispensaries, exclusive sanitariums, city hospitals, and state asylums across the country. Systematic analysis of the published case reports of these treatments offers a new, sometimes surprising, view of the relationship between neurasthenia and the society in which it flourished.

Through a research design that combines a quantitative and qualitative examination of the neurasthenic patient population, content analysis of the journal literature, and a collective biography of the doctors who wrote this literature, I have been able to test previous interpretations and draw broader conclusions about this interesting phenomenon than have heretofore been possible. Chapter 1 describes the development of the neurasthenic model and its earliest proponents. Chapter 2 focuses on the many types of patients diagnosed as neurasthenic and reported on by physicians in the medical journal literature, thus providing an overview of doctors' social and medical views of the disease and demonstrating how widely ideas about the role of emotional and moral factors were accepted. Included in Chapter 2 are rather lengthy passages from medical journal articles describing individual patients. These can be viewed as texts that reveal the remarkable range of conditions physicians diagnosed as neurasthenia, and which, in their care and detail, convey a "feel" for physicians' use of language and for their approach to psychological ailments. For this reason, I thought it best not to paraphrase excessively and to let doctors speak for themselves. The extensive use of case reports in this chapter provides the only collective record of neurasthenic patients, who otherwise would remain anonymous. Chapter 3 explores the perceived symptoms and causes of neurasthenia and examines changes over time in physicians' views on these subjects; Chapter 4 extends this analysis to the methods used to treat neurasthenia. Chapter 5 provides an analysis of both the physician and patient populations associated with neurasthenia, indicating its widespread recognition and social implications. Differences between the various types of practitioners and between male, female, upper-class, and lower-class patients are also explored. The concluding chapter examines the passing of neurasthenia, the coming of Freud, and the place of neurasthenia in the history of psychiatry.

This discussion demonstrates that patient care for nervous diseases in Victorian and Progressive America was on the whole more sensible, and perhaps more effective, than has been recognized. It also reveals how the new science served to justify and reinforce gender and class biases. Yet the fallacies of nineteenth-century psychiatry, when viewed from our modern perspective, should not invoke the feelings of superiority that hindsight usually creates; rather they should alert us to the dangers of being too secure in our own objectivity. Although scientific methods have become more sophisticated in the twentieth century, the story of neurasthenia reminds us that scientists, however objective they strive to be, are nevertheless bound by the cultural restraints of their preconceived values.

NOTES

1. Gerald N. Grob's major studies are *Mental Institutions in America: Social Policy to 1875* (New York: Free Press, 1973), *The State and the Mentally Ill: A History of Worcester State Hospital in Massachusetts, 1830–1920* (Chapel Hill: University of North Carolina Press, 1966), and, most recently, *Mental Illness and American Society, 1875–1940* (Princeton: Princeton University Press, 1983). David Rothman's major works are *Conscience and Convenience: The Asylum and Its Alternatives in Progressive America* (Boston: Little, Brown and Company, 1980) and *The Discovery of the Asylum: Social Order and Disorder in the New Republic* (Boston: Little, Brown and Company, 1971). See also John S. Haller and Robin M. Haller, *The Physician and Sexuality in Victorian America* (Urbana: University of Illinois Press, 1974); and Anita Clair Fellman and Michael Fellman, *Making Sense of Self: Medical Advice Literature in Late Nineteenth-Century America* (Philadelphia: University of Pennsylvania Press, 1981).

2. Perhaps the most notable example of this scholarship is Robert Wiebe's *The Search for Order: 1877–1920* (New York: Hill & Wang, 1967).

3. See, for example, William G. McGloughlin, *The Meaning of Henry Ward Beecher* (New York: Knopf, 1970); Clifford Clark, *Henry Ward Beecher: Spokesman for a Middle-Class America* (Urbana: University of Illinois Press, 1978); and Fellman and Fellman, *Making Sense of Self.*

4. The historiography of neurasthenia is cited in note 1 of Appendix A.

Acknowledgments

In the years that have passed since Wayne Morgan first suggested that I do a study of neurasthenia, I have contracted my fair share of debts. The Graduate School at the University of Oklahoma generously provided me with funds to make an extended research trip to the National Library of Medicine, while the Interlibrary Loan staff at the University of Oklahoma demonstrated remarkable patience in the face of my ever-increasing requests for reprints. A faculty research grant from Vanderbilt University facilitated my work at a critical time and was greatly appreciated.

A number of people deserve thanks for helping me overcome my fear (and ignorance) of statistics and computers, from the 1982 Newberry Library crowd to the staff at the University of Texas Health Science Center at San Antonio's Computing Resources. At the Newberry I benefited most from the help of Marj Murphy, Jan Reiff, Peter Smith, Dan Garside, and my comrades in the class of '82. Roland Wong, Robert Wood, and John Schoolfield, of the Computing Resources staff of the University of Texas Health Science Center at San Antonio, helped "Uncle Skip" through a long, hot summer—and he thanks them for it. In addition, I would like to thank Diane Saucedo for expert data entry, Mary Osborne for writing my format, and Phil VanderMeer for his indispensable help in designing my code. Also, Cindy Gabel and Robert Wood of Computing Resources took great pains to make sure that my tape arrived at the University of Illinois Press in a form that was readable.

Gerald Grob, Charles Rosenberg, James Jones, John Haller, James Whorton, Robert Nye, Steve Kaye, Phil VanderMeer, David Levy, and Antonio Calabria read and commented on the manuscript at various stages. Their suggestions were most helpful. I would like to single out for thanks David R. Johnson of the University of Texas at San Antonio, whose wit and warmth have been an inspiration to numerous scholars who have passed through that institution.

Working with the University of Illinois Press has been a pleasure. Dick Wentworth encouraged my work every step of the way, while Carole Appel made several timely and productive suggestions. I thank them both. In particular I would like to express my appreciation to Patricia Hollahan for editing the manuscript. Pat proved a most understanding editor, though she drew the line when it came to some of my more inventive grammatical turns. My thanks, Pat, for making this a better book.

I have been particularly fortunate in having several close friends to help me with my work when I needed it most. Linda Pritchard has been a colleague's colleague. She has never failed to give me good advice, and her combination of criticism and encouragement has been greatly appreciated—though not always at the time. Don Doyle stuck with me all the way, taking time to read each draft hot off the press. A timely visit to the Doyle clan (Marilyn, Carrie, and Kelly) in Cambridge during some picture-postcard fall weather was instrumental in getting me through the last summer of writing in South Texas. An afternoon spent lounging in front of the Widener with Brazilian cigars and Canadian ales was a cherished memory during some trying (and less decadent) times.

It is with some trepidation that I acknowledge my most substantial debt, for I know it is one that will have to be repaid in kind. This book could not have been written without the contributions of Joyce M. Ray (and, of course, Nathan, who out of sheer boredom memorized the names of my computer files). Those who know me well know how much JR has meant to me and my work. Since now everyone knows, I suppose I will have to work as hard on her book as she has on mine. That's fine with me, for this book—our book—stands as testimony to the life and work we share.

Introduction
Alfred M. Freedman, M.D.

Most contemporary psychiatrists and other mental health professionals accept a certain mythology about the history of American
psychiatry. They tend to believe that modern psychiatry sprang
forth like Pallas Athena from the brow of Zeus when Sigmund
Freud visited the United States and delivered his historic lectures at
Clark University in 1909. Prior to this were the dark ages when
psychiatrists, or alienists as they were then known, limited their
activities to state insane asylums or to private sanitariums far removed from the centers of population.

In this volume, Professor F. G. Gosling not only disposes of the
mythology but gives us new insights into the perturbations of a significant group of nineteenth- and early twentieth-century American patients who suffered from a variety of psychological and psychosomatic maladies. Gosling demonstrates very clearly that in
treating these distressed patients American physicians achieved a
new level of understanding of the relationship between the mind
and the body, that is to say, between mental processes and physical
manifestations. While it is true that other historians have studied
the origins of modern psychiatry prior to Freud's visit to the United
States, their work has been limited primarily to valuable studies of
the asylums to which the mentally ill were committed and of the
philosophy and politics of institutionalization that were involved
in the process. The other significant body of related scholarship

has focused on those who counseled healthy Americans on the achievement of mental equilibrium and social success through correcting unfavorable patterns of living.

Professor Gosling, in a fresh and rewarding approach, has chosen to study a common diagnostic entity known as neurasthenia, which flourished from 1870 to the early part of the twentieth century. Neurasthenia was a catchall diagnosis applied to a syndrome with vague and variable symptoms, particularly manifesting as extreme fatigue, insomnia, depression, headache, dyspepsia, and a variety of nonverifiable physical complaints. Careful examination could reveal no organic basis for these disturbances, but the fact remained that the problems existed and proved incapacitating to individuals who had previously led successful and productive lives.

Neurasthenia was viewed as a single disease by nineteenth-century American physicians. In modern terms, according to the current *Diagnostic and Statistical Manual of Mental Disorders* (*DSM-III*) of the American Psychiatric Association, these cases would for the most part be placed in the diagnostic categories Dysthymic Disorders (Depressive Neuroses), Anxiety Disorders, and Somatoform Disorder. The depression that was almost invariably present would be thought of by many today as a "masked depression," that is, a depressive state that first presents as a physical disorder. Others of these nineteenth-century patients would be thought of in the twentieth century as suffering from psychosomatic disorders of the kind identified as Psychological Factors Affecting Physical Condition. Interestingly enough, although neurasthenia was one of the most common diagnoses made in the late nineteenth century, and still appeared in the last edition of the *Diagnostic and Statistical Manual of Mental Disorders* (*DSM-II*), it was dropped from the *DSM-III* because no one ever used it! Thus, diagnoses based on more specific classification of symptoms have replaced the generic term *neurasthenia,* but the manifestations have remained the same.

In this study Professor Gosling has employed statistical techniques that have been widely utilized by social and political historians; thus his work contributes to a recent movement to bring social history and medical history closer together. In his analysis he measures commonalities and differences between physicians who treated neurasthenia, variables in their views on the disease, and differences between patients. He is thus able to trace over time changes in physicians' perceptions of neurasthenia and to measure changes in beliefs about the management of neurasthenia from its "discovery" in the nineteenth century to its displacement by the dynamic models of twentieth century psychiatry. His statistical delineations allow him to make distinctions regarding the gender and social class of neurasthenic patients—two variables of considerable importance to current social historians. This volume will therefore be of interest not only to practicing health professionals and medical historians but also to historians concerned with class and gender issues. Gosling's use of published case histories from the medical journal literature suggests fruitful possibilities for medical history and for other fields such as women's history.

There are several insights in this volume that should give mental health professionals considerable thought. In the survey of nineteenth-century physicians, we get a good look at their social and moral values. In many respects, the book tells as much about the physicians as about their patients. For example, views of late nineteenth-century physicians toward women are most revealing: women had weaker nervous systems, their lives were governed more by their reproductive organs, and they were in all respects inferior to men. In one case, a doctor attributed the development of neurasthenia in a woman to the fact that she went to college. Other cases of female neurasthenia were attributed to biological causes, since it was thought that woman's physiological makeup and protected social status made her less susceptible to mental overstrain.

Similarly, early descriptions of the disease by its discoverer George Beard and other East Coast neurologists suggested that neurasthenia was a disorder of the urban middle and upper classes. It affected primarily hard-driving, aspiring individuals under great stress who, for some reason, possessed nervous systems that could not withstand the strains of burgeoning American civilization.

This remained a belief because the prominent contributors to the literature, particularly those who wrote for the most influential journals, were the outstanding urban neurologists who saw only such patients in their practices. From Gosling's wide survey it becomes clear that a democratization of neurasthenia occurred and that, as time went on, reports emerged of neurasthenia in laborers, mechanics, farmers, and waitresses. It was thus a physician, not a patient, characteristic that created the myth that only the upper classes suffered from nervous exhaustion. Truly, then, this study relates the social history of a disease, focusing on the characteristics of the physician groups who treated it and the patients who suffered from it.

One of the first facts demonstrated in this study, and one which may surprise modern health care professionals, is that the specialty most concerned and involved with neurasthenia was neurology. The forerunners of today's nervous system specialists were in the nineteenth century much more interested in psychological problems than were the early psychiatrists. It was neurologists who wrote most of the original descriptions of neurasthenia and made major contributions to the diagnosis and treatment of the disorder. The psychiatrists, or alienists as they were called as a result of their work with the "alienated" insane, were occupied for the most part in state mental institutions or private sanitariums. Many of them spent years working in state institutions, sometimes rising to superintendencies or opening their own private hospitals. Pessimistic views of the curability of insanity, coupled with overcrowding and other administrative pressures in state asylums, led to a declining interest in mental therapeutics among asylum superintendents in the late nineteenth century. Interestingly, institutional psychiatrists have continued to place relatively more emphasis on biological factors in mental illness, and many contributions to the somatic treatment of mental disease have come from this branch of psychiatry.

Gosling demonstrates the transformation of etiological concepts of neurasthenia from a somatic disorder with a variety of physical and mental manifestations to the realization that neurasthenia was basically a disorder of the mind. Many physicians, particularly after 1900, spoke of the mind and the body as inseparable and held that perturbations of the mind could produce serious physical symptoms. This process of reversing cause and effect, that is, of changing the perception of mental disturbance from a consequence of organic disorder to a cause of it, in a sense parallels Freud's work. Irritable heart, or DaCosta's Syndrome, for example, was a condition that achieved prominence in nineteenth-century wars, notably the American Civil War, the Franco-Prussian War, and the Boer War. In 1895 Freud wrote a paper, "On the Grounds for Detaching a Particular Syndrome from Neurasthenia under the Description of 'Anxiety Neurosis,'" in which he attributed symptoms that had been described for irritable heart such as "spasms of the heart," "difficulty in breathing," "outbreaks of sweating," and the like as basically anxiety attacks. In his words, "I call this syndrome 'anxiety neurosis' because all its components can be grouped around the chief symptoms of anxiety." Thus, Freud turned DaCosta's Syndrome on its head and, in contrast to previous writers who had attributed the symptoms to a disorder of the heart, emphasized that anxiety was a central unifying factor that produced the somatic manifestations. This is a seminal concept that played a central role in the development of psychiatry and continues to do so.

American neurologists did not use such terms as *actual neurosis* or *psychoneurosis*, but as Gosling shows, they had already formulated concepts that were parallel in many respects to Freud's thinking. Many of the writers on neurasthenia were impressed with the sexual contribution to neurasthenia and described "sexual neurasthenia" as a consequence of masturbation or excessive sexuality. Some of the case histories are remarkably akin to Freud's early descriptions of actual neuroses. It is therefore not surprising that Freud's 1909 Clark University lectures fell upon fertile ground; these were notions that had been widely discussed but never put into the precise and scholarly form that Freud used.

Freud's ideas were not only welcome and congenial to American physicians intellectually, but his Clark lectures meshed very well with basic concepts of American life. America was, and still is, a very pragmatic nation. While theory may be eschewed, something that works is always very appealing. Freud's lectures did not dwell on theory. What he did was to indicate that his theory led to a method—namely, psychoanalysis—and that it worked. This pragmatism contributed in large measure to the wide acceptance of Freudianism in the United States. The American Psychoanalytic Association was founded in 1911 and by 1914 had twenty-three members, most of them elite physicians well positioned to promote the acceptance of Freudian concepts by the medical profession and the American public. Some of these early members, most notably James Jackson Putnam, were neurologists who had contributed significantly to the literature on neurasthenia.

In the 1920s, American psychiatrists young and old traveled to Vienna to study with Freud and his followers. However, as Professor Gosling so well emphasizes, they went with their own intellectual traditions, which had been developed in the late nineteenth and early twentieth centuries. The American form of psychotherapy had been directed mostly toward suggestion and education of the patient. Freud shifted the emphasis from the therapist to the patient; it was the search for self-discovery that finally effected the cure. As Putnam remarked, other therapists told patients, "You can do better if you *try*"; Freud's message was "You can do better if you *know*." Nevertheless, American psychotherapy and psychoanalysis have in many respects incorporated their own educational models into Freud's psychoanalytic knowing model. The educational notion also seems to have influenced many of the neo-Freudians and those who diverged from the classic orthodox model, including many European psychiatrists. Thus, Karen Horney has stated that patients can "be gradually educated to seek to attain the more constructive goals of analytic therapy." Recent trends in psychoanalysis have de-emphasized Freud's model of the analyst as a "blank screen" in favor of a more interactive physician/patient relationship.

Just as the amount of direct analyst involvement desirable in the therapeutic process has occasioned debate within the profession, so has the perceived importance of diagnosis and classification stirred controversy. In the nineteenth century the indiscriminate use of the term neurasthenia raised no eyebrows; it was treatment that concerned American physicians. However, the influence of German nosology, particularly the work of Kraepelin, Freud, and Bleuler, made diagnoses like *hysterical neurasthenia* and *nervous exhaustion* seem nonspecific and misleading in the twentieth century. The preoccupation with nosological systems continued up until World War II, but in the aftermath of the war classification was again seen as relatively unimportant. This was particularly true during the dominance of psychoanalytic approaches, because it appeared that every case required the same treatment. Outstanding psychiatrists such as Karl Menninger proposed that there was only one mental disorder and that classification was irrelevant. Fifteen or twenty years ago one could gather only a handful of people to discuss issues of classification.

With the publication of *DSM-III* classification once again receives great attention and is of considerable concern to the profession. Important social and economic developments, as well as scientific discoveries, have contributed to this renewed interest. Among other factors, the prescribing of psychotropic drugs necessitated careful classification to determine which drug should be used in a particular case. The introduction of health insurance and third-party payments required specific diagnoses to be made in order to obtain reimbursement for services. Diagnoses are scrutinized and might be challenged by various monitoring agencies. Thus we see the interplay of social and economic factors that influence scientific progress, and why some of these achievements are seen in later social milieu as not being advances at all.

It seems that in psychiatry we have moved from one form of reductionism to another. Generally when one uses the term reductionism today, biologic reductionism—the notion that all mental disturbances have a physical origin—comes to mind. In reviewing the development of psychiatry since the nineteenth century, we can see that we have moved through successive periods of reductionism. The years after World War II, particularly from about 1945 to 1960, were a period of psychologic reductionism; psychoanalysis and psychological notions predominated while biological factors were minimized. The view prevailed that psychological means could cure not only all neuroses but also schizophrenia and crime and delinquency. In the writings of nineteenth- and early twentieth-century physicians on neurasthenia one sees quite clearly the concept of wholeness—the assumption that the mind and the body are inseparable. This concept was lost as psychiatry assumed an identity outside of institutions and as Freud's work, with its emphasis on psychological factors, became widely accepted. Opinions such as "if Hitler had been psychoanalyzed, World War II would not have happened" were voiced. Likewise, the 1960s saw a period of social reductionism; if we could only eliminate poverty and bring about social justice, neuroses and psychoses would disappear.

The introduction of psychotropic drugs in the 1950s heralded a resurgence of interest in the biological factors that affect mental processes. Since the 1970s that biological emphasis has dominated psychiatry and has produced dramatic developments in neurochemistry, neurophysiology, brain-imaging, and a variety of other impressive contributions. More recently, however, it is possible to discern a convergence of ideas and the development of what is perhaps an even more promising avenue—an integrative model synthesizing the biological, social, and psychological factors that influence the mind. Is this not in some respects a return to the position of physicians who lived eighty or ninety years ago, but on a sounder scientific basis? It is just possible that we may now be able to develop an improved model of whole behavior that incorporates the strides of the last eighty years but that would also gratify our turn-of-the-century predecessors.

ONE

The Price of Progress

In 1869 a New York neurologist, George M. Beard, coined a term that gave legitimacy to a group of mystifying complaints tormenting the lives of an unknown number of Americans.[1] Beard called this new disease "neurasthenia" (from *neuro* for nerve and *asthenia* for weakness) or "nervous exhaustion."[2] The term has no equivalent in modern medicine, but from the late nineteenth century until Freud's psychological terms were accepted in the 1910s and 1920s, *neurasthenia* was used to characterize practically every nonspecific emotional disorder short of outright insanity, from simple stress to severe neuroses.[3] Neurasthenics were not insane—indeed, many occupied important positions in business and society—but they suffered both mentally and physically. They complained of vague symptoms such as insomnia, headache, fatigue, dyspepsia, depression, and other ailments that prevented them from keeping up their former pace of life.

Three other diagnoses were available for related symptoms complexes, but each had undesirable connotations: hysteria was confined mostly to women and usually involved functional disabilities such as paralysis or loss of feeling; hypochondria entailed imaginary complaints coupled with a desire not to get well; and melancholia implied the presence of delusions. The concepts of psychoanalysis, of course, were unknown, and many physicians bluntly told nervously distraught patients that there was nothing wrong with them except an overactive imagination. Neurasthenia, as envisioned by Beard, was a respectable disease, a functional condition caused by exhaustion of the nerve cells, and its victims truly desired recovery. (Beard indeed believed that he himself had suffered from neurasthenia, and that he had overcome his illness in early adulthood.) Though it sometimes appeared in combination with one of the other neuroses, such as "neurasthenia with hysteria," most physicians believed that the disease did not lead to insanity and, in fact, as a "conservative" neurosis, might prevent it.

Though Beard believed that neurasthenia was a real disease, its actual pathology had not yet been discovered. Lacking empirical evidence to prove neurasthenia's existence, Beard naturally turned to the intellectual authorities of his day to construct an etiology for the disease. Unlike many of his colleagues, Beard never had the opportunity to study abroad. But he read widely, if rather uncritically, and was an admirer of European, and especially German, science.[4] As Charles Rosenberg has pointed out, Beard called with impartiality upon an eclectic group of thinkers and ideas in order to provide "his" disease with scientific credibility. Herbert Spencer, Thomas Edison, and Hermann von Helmholtz gave him "the building blocks with which to construct a mechanistic model explaining the pathology of nervous exhaustion. Du Bois-Reymond supplied proof of the electrical nature of the nervous impulse, Helmholtz and Mayer their work in thermodynamics, Marshall Hall and others the concept of the reflex, and Brown-Séquard 'proof' of the heritability of acquired characteristics." Beard used these ideas "to explain how a disease might be functional and yet as much the product of material change as general paralysis."[5]

By combining social and climatic theories with his scientific speculations, Beard was able to argue that neurasthenia was a preeminently American disease—a product of urban living coupled with the competition of the marketplace and the cool, dry climate of the northeastern United States—and that it was increasing in incidence, particularly among the business and professional men who were most committed to the competitive ethic. It was, in short, the price Americans paid for progress. Women of the "better class" were also prone to the disease because of their more delicate nervous systems; the pressures of running a household or going about in society were likely to cause a breakdown. Being an ardent social Darwinist, Beard drew heavily upon the terminology of evolution in explaining the phenomenon. Arguing that cultural evolution had outstripped the pace of individual evolution, he maintained that specific features of the young American society—in particular the telegraph, the railroads, the periodical press, the sciences, and the atmosphere of political and religious liberty—had increased mental demands on Americans, especially on the urban professionals who labored with their heads rather than their hands. In their attempts to cope with the increased pace of civilization, some of these "brain-workers" exhausted their stock of nerve force and became victims of nervous prostration. Beard believed that neurasthenia was also increasing in the industrialized nations of Europe, but that it would be at least twenty-five years before the incidence of the disease among Europeans approached that already reported in the United States.

Other physicians soon spoke up to confirm Beard's theories, recognizing neurasthenic symptoms in their own patients and adopting his classification. Most of those who became identified as experts on neurasthenia were Beard's colleagues in the American Neurological Association—men like Charles L. Dana, S. Weir Mitchell, A. D. Rockwell, and Henry M. Lyman. These and other neurologists contributed to a better understanding of the causes, diagnosis, progress, and treatment of the disease as they knew it. Lyman, for example, prefaced his review of Beard's *American Nervousness* with a historical overview that explained the great changes wrought by the nineteenth century. The West, he said, had been a wilderness, but "presently there is a cloud of steam in your eyes, and when it is blown away there is no more log cabin or buffalo on the scene." Instead there is "a city of factories and churches and palaces that hides the earth from view. . . . The Arcadian farmer who has been lulled to sleep by the hum of his wife's spinning-wheel is awakened by the shriek of the locomotive."

According to this model, life had gone on for centuries at a slow pace marked by seasonal cycles. Mankind had become accustomed to this leisurely lifestyle and consequently found it difficult to make the transition to modern civilization, with its enormous pressures and demands for constant work. Hence there were new diseases and increased prominence of certain varieties of disease as a result of imperfect adjustment to the enormous change in the conditions of life. "In other words," Lyman wrote, "the incidents which constitute existence have been so greatly multiplied by the intervention of steam-power and electricity that without a corresponding increase in the power of grasping and corrolating [*sic*] those incidents, the apparatus for their apprehension and coordination (the brain and the nerves) must necessarily suffer from excessive and inappropriate use. The pretty little piece of machinery which suffices for a pleasure-boat on a pond," Lyman maintained, "would soon break down in an attempt to drive an ocean-steamer through a storm. This sudden transformation has been the fate . . . of the present generation of Americans: hence the great variety and severity of nervous disorders among this class."[6]

Lyman's was a simplified description of Beard's theory of neurasthenic causation. Beard, in fact, devised an elaborate algebraic formula to account for the dramatic increase of nervousness in urban America: it was, he thought, "civilization in general [and] American civilization in particular (young and rapidly growing nation, with civil, religious, and social liberty) . . . exhausting climate (extremes of heat and cold, and dryness) . . . the nervous diathesis . . . [and] overwork or overworry, or excessive indulgence of appetites or passions [that resulted in] an attack of neurasthenia or nervous exhaustion."[7]

Almost fifteen years after Lyman's review, Beard's colleague A. D. Rockwell offered an explanation of neurasthenia that still borrowed heavily from Beard's vocabulary. "In the older countries," Rockwell held, "men plod along in the footsteps of their fathers, generation after generation, with little possibility and therefore little thought of entering a higher social grade. Here, on the contrary, no one is content to rest with the possibility ever before him of stepping higher, and the race of life is all haste and unrest. It is thus readily seen," Rockwell asserted, "that the primary cause of neurasthenia in this country is civilization itself, with all that the term implies, with its railway, telegraph, telephone, and periodical press intensifying in ten thousand ways cerebral activity and worry."[8]

So successful was this explanation that neurasthenia, or "nervousness," was to become turn-of-the-century America's primary mental disorder that still fell short of insanity, and a disease symbolically identified with the period. If not an epidemic, at least it seemed to be increasing at an alarming rate. By 1900 a substantial body of literature on the disease had appeared in textbooks, medical journals, and popular periodicals across the country. Neurasthenia reached its peak of popularity in the early years of the new century and began to decline after 1910. By the 1920s it had been all but forgotten as new concepts of neuroses and psychoses came to be increasingly accepted in both the United States and Europe.

One of the reasons for the demise of neurasthenia as a diagnostic concept was the failure of its proponents to discover the pathological basis of the disease—a physical cause that virtually every practitioner believed to exist and that the scientific thinking of the period demanded. But it is the lack of a clear pathological origin that makes neurasthenia so interesting to the historian. Because so little was known of the ailment, physicians relied heavily on their own cultural biases and preconceived opinions to expound on what they took to be scientific facts and objective observations. Thus the body of neurasthenic literature provides a fascinating glimpse not only of the last pre-Freudian medical generation but of the first generation of Americans to be confronted with the new technologies and social patterns of industrial America.

The popular view of psychiatry is that the specialty arose with Freud, and that before the twentieth century neuroses were unrecognized and psychoses untreated. Even medical historians, who know that the picture is far more complex, have associated psychological treatments primarily with alienists and neurologists, and neurasthenia with the elite urban neurologists who were members of the ANA. Analysis of the entirety of the neurasthenic literature, however, leads to a fuller interpretation of the disease, one that recognizes that the term *neurasthenia* gave expression to a pervasive need existing among people of all social classes for psychological and emotional support from their doctors. The physicians who treated neurasthenia represented a broad spectrum of differing specialties, career patterns, and medical viewpoints. What they shared was a concern for the emotional health of their patients.

Clearly, many physicians echoed Beard's contention that neurasthenia resulted from the pace of American civilization and found expression in a wide variety of subjective mental symptoms. Beard himself provided the most complete list of neurasthenic symptoms ever compiled, thereby ensuring that almost any complaint not specifically attached to another known disease could be diagnosed as some form of neurasthenia. In the spirit of thoroughness characteristic of Beard's work, *American Nervousness* included a list of symptoms fully two pages in length. This list, he cautioned, was "only representative and typical," for "an absolutely exhaustive catalogue . . . cannot be prepared, since every case differs somewhat from every other case." He listed "insomnia, flushing, drowsiness, bad dreams, cerebral irritation, dilated pupils, pain, pressure and heaviness in the head, changes in the expression of the eye, neurasthenic asthenopia, noises in the ears, atonic voice, mental irritability, tenderness of the teeth and gums, nervous dyspepsia, desire for stimulants and narcotics, abnormal dryness of the skin, joints and mucous membranes, sweating hands and feet with redness . . . , fear of lightning, or fear of responsibility, of open places or of closed places, fear of society, fear of being alone, fear of fears, fear of contamination, fear of everything, deficient mental control, lack of decision in trifling matters, hopelessness, deficient thirst and capacity for assimilating fluids, . . . pains in the back, heaviness of the loins and limbs, shooting pains . . . , cold hands and feet, pain in the feet, . . . special idiosyncracies in regard to food, medicines, and external irritants, local spasms of muscles, difficulty of swallowing, convulsive movements, especially on going to sleep, cramps, a feeling of profound exhaustion . . . ," and a host of other chills, pains, obsessions, and itches.[9]

The all-encompassing nature of the neurasthenic model was valuable to nineteenth-century physicians, who first had to understand symptomatic relationships before they could subdivide them into more distinct categories. Even Sigmund Freud, trained as a neurologist, considered himself neurasthenic early in his career, though his later theories of the id, ego, and superego were far more complex models of the inner workings of the mind than the simple single-disease concept of neurasthenia. But while the twentieth century's more sophisticated view showed neurasthenia to be nothing more than a crude collage of symptoms having only a tenuous relationship, it was the recognition that these symptoms were somehow related—however loosely—that made the term useful to nineteenth-century physicians. The awareness that mental disturbances could be associated with disease that was neither insanity nor organic illness gave neurasthenia its diagnostic value.

The list of neurasthenics who were well known in American intellectual circles included William and Alice James, Charlotte Perkins Gilman, and Jane Addams. Abroad, the names of Charles Darwin, Herbert Spencer, George Eliot, Rousseau, Montaigne, Francis Bacon, and Kant were counted among the victims.[10] Beard estimated that 10 percent of his patient load was made up of fellow physicians; clearly one could be diagnosed as neurasthenic and still hold up one's head in society. Most Americans agreed with Beard that they were making a sacrifice so that others could enjoy the fruits of their labors. They believed that their own modern culture was the most stressful that had ever existed, or probably would exist again, in this period that the Hallers have termed "the nervous century."[11]

Beyond the concerns of these elites, who perhaps exaggerated their own importance, were countless men and women who suffered not from overexcitement but from grief, depression, anxiety, and the overwhelming tedium of their lives. They too were neurasthenics, but they were more likely to visit a general practitioner than one of the high-priced neurologists who practiced in the major cities of the United States. While we know very little about these men and women, we do know something about the physicians who treated them and who wrote about their findings in the medical journals of the period. This literature, as well as the writings of the famous neurologists, draws a portrait of the American medical community's perceptions of itself, its patients, and its times as these related to the question of nervousness in society at large. Lesser-known physicians looked to their more prestigious colleagues for the construction of a theoretical model of neurasthenia, but they were also influenced by their own experiences and the needs of their own patients in treating the suffering that nervousness produced.

The neurologists whose names came to be most closely associated with neurasthenia were members of an elite group who derived much of their status and income from treating the upper-middle-class patients who could best afford care for such subjective symptoms. The neurological specialty developed first in Europe and gained momentum in this country when the Civil War underscored the need for physicians to treat nerve injuries, battle fatigue, and shell shock, as well as to distinguish emotional distress from malingering. Indicative of neurologists' status is the fact that incomes for at least some members of this group exceeded $50,000 a year by the 1870s.[12]

The most influential of the early neurologists were members of the American Neurological Association, one of the first specialty medical societies in the United States. Thirty-five neurologists met in New York City in June of 1875 to form the association in response to a letter sent out the previous year by seven physicians: William A. Hammond, Meredith Clymer, Edward C. Seguin, and T. M. B. Cross of New York; James S. Jewell of Chicago; James Jackson Putnam of Boston; and Roberts Bartholow of Cincinnati. These neurologists lived primarily in major cities like Philadelphia, New York, and Boston, with a few living in Chicago and St. Louis. They were particularly aggressive in defending their specialty and eager to achieve legitimacy in treating nervous and mental disorders.[13] Neurologists tended to look for scientific guidance from the Continent, where many of them had done postgraduate work. As Charles Rosenberg notes, "their adherence to the aspirations of world science—like the process of specialization itself—foreshadowed the development of modern medicine in the United States."[14] By the time Beard first published on neurasthenia, better methods of cell staining and improved microscopy techniques were making clear the role of cells in the nervous system. It was known that the cerebral cortex responded to electrical stimulation, and researchers were close to discovering the neuron. Optimism prevailed in the neurological and neurophysiological communities.[15]

The neurologists of the late nineteenth century had little in common with their present-day namesakes. They were a curious blend of physician, psychiatrist, and anatomist, and, except for those who limited their practices to organic disorders such as epilepsy and nerve injuries, they were much nearer to being forerunners of twentieth-century psychiatrists than of modern neurologists because of their emphasis on the emotions and the social origins of stress. The lack of scientific knowledge of pathology and physiology in the period prevented them from doing much more than treating the external manifestations of disease, and they were anxious to add mental complaints to their repertoire. The acceptance of neurasthenia as a legitimate if not well-understood disease helped to fill waiting rooms with patients who might otherwise have suffered quietly in shame and fear, complained to family physicians, or even sought help from one of the nonmedical healing cults.

The period from 1870 to 1910 witnessed the rise to dominance, the subsequent state of crisis, and the eventual decline of the somatic style in medicine, which required that a lesion be present for a state of disease to exist.[16] As Nathan Hale notes, however, "the apparently precise word lesion embraced a multitude of conditions, including 'structural,' [and] 'functional.' Structural lesions represented permanent, ascertainable changes in tissue. Functional lesions could not be detected by known methods," but physicians expected to find them in short order.[17] In practice, then, somaticism made a distinction between organic ailments exhibiting anatomical change and functional ailments resulting from physiological processes, a crucial if somewhat artificial distinction that allowed physicians to incorporate neurasthenia into the prevailing medical model even though its pathology was not yet known.[18] As Hale observes, the failure to find lesions did not deter neurologists, who "argued that the very fact that patients still functioned in most important ways proved that the lesions were subtle and complex and would be found by new methods."[19]

The search for methods that could pinpoint localized lesions in functional conditions like neurasthenia inevitably led neurologists to create entirely speculative pathologies.[20] Since researchers could not observe living human tissue in order to discover convolutions of the brain or other abnormalities that might explain mental disorders, much attention was paid to the examination of brain matter at autopsies. Those of criminals and the certified insane, whose brains would certainly exhibit the greatest pathological deviations, were given the most careful attention. Most neurologists, however, busied themselves with the urgent needs of their living patients and left the research to physiologists and asylum physicians, who had more readily available subjects.

Given the absence of any real scientific breakthroughs in the understanding of mental diseases comparable to the discoveries made possible by the advent of the germ theory, it is little wonder that neurologists were eager to accept neurasthenia as a discrete disease entity. This, at least, imposed an external order on otherwise inexplicable phenomena. As time went by and the pathological basis of neurasthenia and other functional neuroses remained obscure, a crisis developed in the somatic style of medicine and a new generation of mental therapists challenged all elements of the somatic paradigm. While efforts to create neurophysiological and psychopharmacological theories and therapies continued and led to experimentation with somatically oriented psychiatric treatments like lobotomy and insulin shock, the search for a pathology of functional ailments like neurasthenia was largely abandoned with the triumph of Freudian thinking in American neurology. The search has been renewed recently in the field of biomedical psychiatry, which has focused its efforts on discovering the physical and genetic bases of mental illness. But as Hale points out, even "Freud's psychoanalysis in many respects remained a theory rooted in the body and in the psychological consequences of physical functions and attributes."[21]

The absence of a pathological model served to blur the theoretical distinctions between physicians of various stripes and led to occasionally intense internal rivalry. Professional competition was widespread, as new specialties tried to establish their own turf in competition with the time-honored family physician. Neurologists, because of the nebulous character of their sphere, had to fend off challenges from a variety of other groups—both within and outside of the medical profession—to establish their own domain. Thus they found themselves at odds with general practitioners and competing medical specialists, as well as with mind curists, hypnotists, and Christian Scientists.

The neurologists' chief rivals in the psychiatric field were the alienists, an earlier generation of mental therapists whose field was primarily treatment of the insane. Alienists, so called because they treated the misfits who were "alienated" from society, traced their origins to the perfectionist climate of Jacksonian America in the 1830s and 1840s, when it was thought that simple humane care and "moral" treatment could cure mental illness and educate the insane to mental health.[22] As Nancy Tomes has pointed out, moral treatment was "inspired by a more optimistic view of human nature, which had roots in both the secular humanism of the Enlightenment and the pietistic doctrine of evangelicalism . . . [and] appealed to the lunatics' supposedly innate capacity to live a moral, ordered existence."[23] The first generation of alienists, in fact, was made up of concerned laymen who essentially acted as missionaries to the insane and who believed that the key to treatment lay merely in the setting of a good example. The placement of asylums in remote rural areas was thought to contribute to the creation of a therapeutic environment—a theory which conveniently coincided with the availability of cheap land. The alienists had professionalized in 1844 with the founding of the Association of Medical Superintendents of American Institutions for the Insane (AMSAII) in Philadelphia. Thirteen of the country's most prominent alienists, including Isaac Ray, Samuel B. Woodward, Thomas S. Kirkbride, and Amariah Brigham, who founded the *American Journal of Insanity,* were founding members.[24]

For some three decades before the founding of the ANA, then,

these medical superintendents—speaking through the AMSAII—
had been the undisputed authorities on matters pertaining to the
mind and its disorders. But by the 1870s the alienists found themselves in a beleaguered position. Cure rates reported in the early
asylum years proved to be inflated, and declining success in the
treatment of insanity gave rise to more pessimistic theories that
heavily emphasized heredity. If insanity was hereditary and therefore organic in origin, nothing could be done to treat its victims
until its underlying pathology was discovered. By this time asylums
were so overcrowded that they were able to offer little more than
custodial care, and superintendents often spent as much time lob-
bying state legislatures for funds or attending to administrative
concerns as they did on medical matters.[25] Physicians were promoted only from within, and the system attracted only those willing to serve lengthy apprenticeships as assistant superintendents
before getting the chance to take over their own institutions. The
remote location of many asylums was now seen as a drawback, as
it deterred physicians who sought stimulating social and professional contacts and lucrative private practices. Thus, the AMSAII
remained a closed group dominated by a small number of asylum
heads—assistant superintendents and superintendents of institutions for the feebleminded were not admitted to membership—
and ambitious young physicians interested in the field of nervous
and mental diseases became increasingly attracted to the growing
specialty of neurology.

By the late 1870s the conflict between alienists and neurologists
had become heated. At issue was the question of which experts
would be recognized as public spokesmen on matters relating to
mental health and illness. One of the first manifestations of the
conflict was the New York Neurological Society's petition to the
New York legislature in 1878 asking for an investigation of conditions in the state's asylums, a move aimed at giving neurologists
access to patients and control over clinical matters.[26] Dr. Edward
C. Spitzka, a young German-trained neuroanatomist who was a
moving force in the New York society, attacked alienists in general
and Dr. John P. Gray, longtime editor of the AMSAII's official pub-

lication, the *American Journal of Insanity,* and superintendent of the Utica Asylum for the Insane since 1850, in particular. Spitzka accused the superintendents of "scientific incompetence, extravagance, and religious bigotry . . . [and] abuse of patients and the juggling of financial accounts." He labeled Gray "an indifferent, superficial man, owing his position merely to political buffoonery." Gray and the superintendents easily weathered this first frontal attack because of their close and friendly connections with Albany legislators and the investigation had little effect on asylum conditions, but the alienists increasingly had to share the public spotlight with their neurological opponents.[27]

The most celebrated insanity trial of the nineteenth century—that of Charles Guiteau, the accused assassin of President James Garfield—showcased the conflict between neurologists and the asylum superintendents and demonstrated the profound social and philosophical differences between the two groups. Spitzka served as expert witness for Guiteau's defense; the government countered by employing Gray for the prosecution. The trial, which took place in late 1881 and early 1882, featured Spitzka arguing that though Guiteau might seem rational according to his own delusional scheme, he was still insane and hence not responsible for his actions. Gray, on the other hand, testified that Guiteau "understood the nature and consequences of his act, appeared to reason coherently, and hence, following the generally accepted rule of law, was guilty."[28] Gray further explained the traditional view that the only possible manifestations of insanity were mania, melancholia, and dementia; as Guiteau exhibited none of these symptoms, he could not be insane.

Guiteau's behavior before and during the trial reveal him to have been insane by contemporary standards—probably a paranoid schizophrenic. He claimed that he had been only temporarily insane at the time of the shooting because he was being used as an instrument of God "in the employ of Jesus Christ and Company." He expected not only exoneration but appointment to an important post in the Arthur administration. Many neurologists pleaded for leniency in the face of such obvious disturbance, but the conservative view of the superintendents prevailed and Guiteau was convicted and executed in 1882.[29]

Neurologists also found themselves in competition with specialists outside of the psychiatric field. These disputes were primarily economic and involved competition for patients who exhibited symptoms of neurasthenia but who might actually be suffering from some undiscovered local condition such as an ovarian cyst or even eyestrain. Gynecologists especially waged war with neurologists because of the accepted belief in the close relationship between a woman's reproductive organs and her nervous system.[30] Medical specialization paralleled the growing division of labor in society at large; numerous technical innovations during the latter part of the century made it possible to examine specific organs of the body with increased precision. Gynecologists, through examination of the female reproductive system, often discovered abnormalities which might account for their patients' nervousness, and they consequently claimed that neurologists treated women for mental disorders that were often of discoverable pathological origin. Since, however, most uterine and ovarian disorders could not be detected without surgery, neurologists countered that numerous women were being subjected to unneccessary and dangerous operations by their gynecologists; these operations, if anything, left them more nervous than before.

The neurologist James G. Kiernan, professor of forensic psychiatry at Kent College of Law, expressed a common criticism of gynecological localism when he remarked upon the "evil effects of laying undue stress on the utero-ovarian manifestation." Kiernan held that gynecologists' preoccupation with locating symptoms in the reproductive organs had the ultimate effect of burdening patients with "new material for morbid anxieties."[31] Radical gynecological surgery—especially ovariotomies and clitoridectomies—bore the major brunt of neurologists' criticism.

Some charges were quite damning. The outspoken Ludwig Bremer of St. Louis, in an article published in the *Journal of Nervous and Mental Disease* (the official journal of the ANA), went so far as to argue that gynecologists' "craving for surgical interference about the genital sphere . . ." constituted a threat to the institution of marriage. Bremer, who championed what he called a "rational general plan of treatment" for functional ailments like neurasthenia, charged that "gynecological treatment . . . is a crime, that its effect upon the woman is that of defloration. Her moral tone, her manner of judging things is altered and lowered; with the consciousness of there being even the shadow of a flaw on her virginity, those subtle qualities disappear which constitute the charm of girlish innocence; her mind is polluted, she is unfit for marriage, and all this because her doctor happens to hold the opinion that by manipulating the uterus he can cure neuroses."

Bremer noted that the modern woman more often sought marital advice from a gynecologist than from a minister, and he pictured the unfortunate result: "All her thinking becomes concentrated on her womb, her egotism . . . assumes immense proportions," and "in the worst cases [she] worships her doctor as her hero and benefactor." The marriage of such a woman was doomed, for "the continued doctor's bills are far from having a soothing influence on the mind of the disgruntled husband, who sees through this farce and conceives an inextinguishable loathing for his wife. The finale of the drama is enacted in the courts under the designation of cruelty, neglect and incompatability of temper." [32]

In light of accusations that they deflowered young women and broke up marriages, it would have been surprising indeed if gynecologists had not risen to the defense of their therapeutic philosophy. The most common response was to praise radical surgery as a revolutionary step in medical history. David Todd Gilliam, in an article that appeared in the *Transactions of the American Association of Obstetricians, Gynecologists, and Abdominal Surgeons* in 1896, expressed a widely held attitude when he maintained that "women are by nature more nearly neutral than men, and the deprivation of the sexual glands is less felt by them, and . . . I have seen many instances in which castration has been followed by a marked change in disposition and temper, and always for the better." [33] E. Arnold Praeger of Los Angeles went beyond the biological arguments advanced in defense of radical surgery in an

1895 article in the *Transactions*. According to Praeger (a zealous advocate of female surgery),

> the charge brought against us of seeking to short-cut our way to fame is very wide of the mark, because the moment the people find that a surgeon is what they are pleased to call "fond of the knife," his usefulness is likely to be seriously impaired. . . . Were we anxious to retaliate for the many hard knocks dealt to us as gynecologists, we should not have very hard work to prove that as many have fallen victims to new drugs and new-fashioned theories in medicine without any pathological facts to support them as can be laid to the charge of the . . . gynecologist; while if we were to take into account the sins of omission of our ultra-conservative friends and attempt to count those whose lives were sacrificed to prejudice . . . , we should have such a heavy balance in our favor that some of our ultra-conservative critics would in all probability look about for some other material from which to construct their papers for some time to come. . . . Were it not for the "enthusiasts" medicine and surgery would not have made the rapid strides with which they are rightly credited.[34]

Praeger's spirited defense of gynecological surgery was perhaps directed not so much at competing specialists as at another, larger group who opposed the idea of specialization itself. These were the general practitioners who, understandably enough, feared that the move toward specialization threatened their own economic well-being. The traditional role of the general practitioner was one of confidant and counselor as well as physician, a responsibility that called for the doctor to minister to a wide variety of physical and emotional ills. General practitioners placed a heavy emphasis on the development of close relationships with individual patients. Before the mid-twentieth century, when specific remedies for identified diseases began to characterize medical practice, moral support and encouragement often provided the major form of treatment, and these commodities general practitioners considered themselves best able to provide.

General practitioners frequently attacked specialization because they believed it led to a too-heavy concentration on local manifestations at the expense of concern for the patient's overall condition (an issue raised again more recently by those who fear a growing trend toward overspecialization). Thus general practitioners found themselves both in agreement with and in conflict with neurologists. On the one hand, they, like neurologists, were concerned with the patient's "tone," meaning both physical and emotional health; on the other hand, they felt competent to treat both and saw no reason to give up the mental aspect of their practices to specialists.

Specialization was most pronounced in urban areas and made little headway in rural communities, where the general practitioner remained the dominant fixture. Even in major cities like New York it was not uncommon for physicians to receive all patients who called upon them, regardless of their area of specialization.[35] Many physicians were specialists in name only, and, unless they identified themselves as such by joining a specialty society or studying with acknowledged leaders in the field, it is difficult to determine whether or not they limited their practices to certain diseases or parts of the anatomy. Nonetheless, specialization was the prevailing trend, and its advantages and disadvantages were hotly debated in medical journals, many of which served as mouthpieces for practitioners of competing therapeutic persuasions. General practitioners' fears that specialists would drive them into extinction appeared to be well founded, and despite their opposition, the move toward specialization continued.[36]

The literature on neurasthenia offers insight into physicians' views on specialization. It also sheds new light on physicians' gender and class assumptions about patients, and the effects of these attitudes on diagnosis and treatment, as well as on the development of the fields of psychiatry and psychology. This literature provides new evidence about a strange "disease" that disappeared after capturing the imagination of a medical generation, a disease that seems to have been no more than a foolish fad yet is somehow disturbingly familiar in our own time. Its supposed prevalence and the concerns that it generated remind us that we are not the first age to experience stress and psychic pain. The arrogance of our presumption that our own "modern" civilization is both the most advanced and the most psychologically difficult is demonstrated quite clearly by the testimony of those who reached an identical conclusion about their own time a century ago.

NOTES

1. George M. Beard, "Neurasthenia, or Nervous Exhaustion," *Boston Medical and Surgical Journal*, 80 (1869), 245–59. Actually the term *neurasthenia* had been used prior to Beard's article, but he was the first to describe it as a clinical entity. Beard's books on the subject did not appear until some years later: *A Practical Treatise on Nervous Exhaustion (Neurasthenia): Its Symptoms, Nature, Sequences, Treatment* (New York: Wood, 1880) and *American Nervousness, Its Causes and Consequences* (New York: G. P. Putnam's Sons, 1881). The former described the disease clinically, while the latter, which has become a minor medical classic, dealt with etiology. See Charles E. Rosenberg, "The Place of George M. Beard in Nineteenth-Century Psychiatry," *Bulletin of the History of Medicine*, 36 (1962), 248.

2. Beard did not invent the term *neurasthenia*, though he was given credit for describing the disorder more scientifically than anyone before him. Among those who traced the term further back was Dr. George W. Johnston of Washington, D.C. In a discussion following Dr. Francis B. Bishop's paper on neurasthenia in 1897, Johnston noted that the term appeared in *Dunglison's Dictionary* in 1833, "side by side with its German equivalent, Nervenschwache." Johnston eventually traced the term back to an 1814 medical dictionary and to a work of Gianini, a professor in Milan, published in 1808. Francis B. Bishop, "Nervousness," *Transactions of the Medical Society of the District of Columbia*, 1897, pp. 379–80. The contention over the origin of the term does not change the fact that most physicians believed Beard to have provided it with more meaning than his predecessors had.

3. The term *neurasthenic neurosis* appeared in the American Psychiatric Association's second edition of the *Diagnostic and Statistical Manual of Mental Disorders* in 1968 as a condition characterized "by complaints of chronic weakness, easy fatigability, and sometimes exhaustion" (pp. 40–41). By the time the third edition was issued in 1980, however, neurasthenia had again dropped out of the nomenclature. It is simply

listed in the index as a "see" reference to Dysthymic Disorders, which are characterized by "features of the depressive syndrome, but . . . not of sufficient severity and duration to meet the criteria for a major depressive episode" (p. 213).

4. For a discussion of the importance of German science in American medicine in the late nineteenth century, see Kenneth M. Ludmerer, *Learning to Heal: The Development of American Medical Education* (New York: Basic Books, Inc., 1985), esp. pp. 29–38.

5. Rosenberg, "Place of George M. Beard," p. 249.

6. Henry M. Lyman, "Nervous Disorders in America," *Dial*, 2 (1881), 81–82.

7. Beard, *American Nervousness*, p. 176.

8. A. D. Rockwell, "Some Causes and Characteristics of Neurasthenia," *New York Medical Journal*, 58 (1893), 590.

9. Beard, *American Nervousness*, pp. viii–ix.

10. Haller and Haller, *Physician and Sexuality*, p. 8.

11. This is the title of the first chapter of *Physician and Sexuality*, pp. 3–43.

12. Bonnie Ellen Blustein, "New York Neurologists and the Specialization of American Medicine," *Bulletin of the History of Medicine*, 53 (1979), 172, and Barbara Sicherman, "The Uses of a Diagnosis: Doctors, Patients, and Neurasthenia," *Journal of the History of Medicine*, 32 (1977), 40.

13. For more on neurology during this period see Charles E. Rosenberg, *The Trial of the Assassin Guiteau: Psychiatry and Law in the Gilded Age* (Chicago: University of Chicago Press, 1968), pp. 60–74; Blustein, "New York Neurologists," pp. 170–83; Blustein, "A New York Medical Man: William Alexander Hammond (1828–1900), Neurologist," (Ph.D. dissertation, University of Pennsylvania, 1979); Andrew Abbott, "The Evolution of American Psychiatry, 1880–1930" (Ph.D. dissertation, University of Chicago, 1982); and Sicherman, "Uses of a Diagnosis," pp. 33–54.

14. Rosenberg, *Trial of the Assassin Guiteau*, p. 60.

15. Eric T. Carlson, "George M. Beard and Neurasthenia," in Edward R. Wallace IV and Lucius C. Pressley, eds., *Essays in the History of Psychiatry* (Columbia, S.C.: Wm. S. Hall Psychiatric Institute, 1980), pp. 50–51.

16. For a lengthy and detailed account of the rise and decline of the somatic style see Nathan G. Hale, Jr., *Freud and the Americans: The Beginnings of Psychoanalysis in the United States, 1876–1917* (New York: Oxford University Press, 1971), especially pp. 47–97. As Hale states, "because of the large proportion of non-scientific elements in neurology

and psychiatry, 'style' is an appropriate term for a consistent approach usually based on a distinctive model and a related set of hypotheses" (p. 48).

17. Ibid., p. 51.

18. Rosenberg, "Place of George M. Beard," p. 249.

19. Hale, *Freud and the Americans,* p. 52.

20. Ibid.

21. Ibid., p. 73.

22. This discussion is condensed from J. M. Ray and F. G. Gosling, "Historical Perspectives on the Treatment of Mental Illness in the United States," *Journal of Psychiatry and Law,* 10 (1982), 135–61.

23. Nancy Tomes, *A Generous Confidence: Thomas Story Kirkbride and the Art of Asylum-Keeping, 1840–1883* (Cambridge: Cambridge University Press, 1984), p. 5. While it has been common to regard American alienism as dependent upon ideas developed by Phillipe Pinel in France and the Quaker William Tuke in England, Tomes argues that the physicians who first practiced moral treatment at the Pennsylvania Hospital in the late 1700s were apparently unaware of European developments until the early 1800s. See Tomes's introduction, particularly pp. 4–5, for the development of this argument.

24. See Grob, *Mental Institutions in America,* pp. 132–73, for the founding of the AMSAII. See also John A. Pitts, "The Association of Medical Superintendents of American Institutions for the Insane, 1844–1892: A Case Study of Specialism in American Medicine" (Ph.D. dissertation, University of Pennsylvania, 1978), and, for a study that carries the story into the twentieth century, Abbott, "Evolution of American Psychiatry."

25. For an analysis of how asylums changed between the founding generation and the later 1800s, see, for a public asylum, Gerald N. Grob, *The State and the Mentally Ill: A History of Worcester State Hospital in Massachusetts, 1830–1920* (Chapel Hill: University of North Carolina Press, 1966), and, for a private (corporate) institution, Tomes, *Generous Confidence.*

26. For more on this confrontation, see Bonnie Ellen Blustein, "'A Hollow Square of Psychological Science': American Neurologists and Psychiatrists in Conflict," in Edward Scull, ed., *Madhouses, Mad-Doctors, and Madmen: The Social History of Psychiatry in the Victorian Era* (Philadelphia: University of Pennsylvania Press, 1981), pp. 241–70.

27. Rosenberg, *Trial of the Assassin Guiteau,* p. 72.

28. Ibid., p. xiv.

29. The full story of the Guiteau trial, and its relationship to late nine-

teenth-century American culture and medicine, is told in Rosenberg, *Trial of the Assassin Guiteau.*

30. There was a great deal of overlap in the positions of neurologists and gynecologists on the cause and effect of neurasthenia, but the two groups of specialists tended to emphasize their differences, aware of the economic stakes involved. For more detail on the competition between neurologists and gynecologists—and genitourinary surgeons—see F. G. Gosling and J. M. Ray, "The Right to Be Sick: American Physicians and Nervous Patients, 1885–1910," *Journal of Social History,* 20 (1986), 251–67.

31. James G. Kiernan, "Inter-Complications of Neurasthenia," *Journal of the American Medical Association,* 29 (1897), 583.

32. Ludwig Bremer, "On the Reflex Theory in Nervous Disease," *Journal of Nervous and Mental Disease,* 17 (1892), 575.

33. David Todd Gilliam, "Oophorectomy for the Insanity and Epilepsy of the Female: A Plea for Its More General Adoption," *Transactions of the American Association of Obstetricians, Gynecologists, and Abdominal Surgeons,* 9 (1896), 319.

34. E. Arnold Praeger, "Is So-Called Conservatism in Gynecology Conducive of the Best Results for the Patient?" *Transactions of the American Association of Obstetricians, Gynecologists, and Abdominal Surgeons,* 8 (1895), 323.

35. Charles E. Rosenberg, "The Practice of Medicine in New York a Century Ago," *Bulletin of the History of Medicine,* 41 (1967), 249.

36. A good introduction to late nineteenth-century specialization is William G. Rothstein, *American Physicians in the Nineteenth Century: From Sects to Science* (Baltimore: The Johns Hopkins University Press, 1972), pp. 198–213.

TWO

Nerve Invalids All

In the fall of 1871 George Beard was called by Dr. H. W. Thayer of Brooklyn to consult on a case involving a twenty-seven-year-old merchant. Mr. W—— was suffering from "general debility," fatigue, weakness, transient numbness, weakness of the bladder, dyspepsia, insomnia, and, at times, mental depression; Beard also noted that when the patient put his left hand in warm water it "felt very disagreeable." The patient had traveled to Europe in an effort to cure himself, but had returned rather worse than better. "Long standing in picture galleries," Beard observed, "seemed to have aggravated all the symptoms." The diagnosis was neurasthenia, Beard's only question being whether to call the case simple spinal congestion (myelasthenia) or myelasthenia complicated by cerebrasthenia. Beard thought the illness caused by overwork and "perhaps excessive use of the sexual organs" acting on a nervous constitution.

The case of Mr. W—— is that of a stereotypical neurasthenic patient: a businessman of some means, in the prime of young adulthood, but with an inherited nervousness that produced or intensified otherwise unremarkable symptoms. The seemingly minor complaints somehow made this young man miserable enough to seek treatment, in fact to spend several months in Europe trying to relieve his condition before seeing Dr. Thayer. His case was considered serious enough to warrant a consultation with one of the country's leading neurologists.

The reporting of patient cases makes clear that neurologists associated with the American Neurological Association (ANA) were the leaders in advising on the diagnosis and treatment of neurasthenia; they reported fully two-thirds of the patients for whom sufficient data was given. Of the 307 individual neurasthenics described in medical journals between 1870 and 1910, 205 were patients of ANA neurologists, twenty-eight of independent neurologists (not members of the ANA), and seventy-four of non-neurologists.[1] Most cases were cited to illustrate typical symptoms and causes of nervous exhaustion or to demonstrate effective treatments, though occasional reports described unusual or difficult cases. General practitioners, non-neurological specialists, and those neurologists who were not members of the ANA were much more likely than ANA members were to describe only a single patient or to report no cases. The ANA neurologists' superiority of numbers in reporting cases suggests their own perception that they were the authorities in the field of nervous disorders.

Given that neurasthenia has been associated by historians primarily with the upper classes, the diversity of the patient population reported in the medical journal literature is surprising; nervous Americans represented a spectrum of occupations from farmers to bank presidents.[2] Of the 217 patients whose occupations were given, seventy-nine were of the professional class, including bankers, engineers, lawyers, merchants, clergymen, politicians, physicians, and university faculty, as well as a newspaper editor, a hospital superintendent, and various other men of some distinction. But though theirs was the largest identifiable group, members of the wealthy and upper middle class by no means accounted for the majority of patients cited in the literature. Fifty-six patients belonged to the skilled and semiskilled laboring classes that made up a large part of the nineteenth-century work force; among them were bookkeepers, bank tellers, butchers, carpenters, clerks, storekeepers, tailors, and masters of such uncommon skills

Table 1. Patient Occupations

	Percent of Total	N
Professional	36.4	79
Skilled/Semiskilled	25.8	56
Housewives	20.3	44
Laborers	9.7	21
Other	7.8	17
	100.0	217

as wire weaving and brass polishing.[3] Twenty-one patients were of the unskilled laboring class, including waiters, waitresses, servants and housekeepers, a "car cleaner," a stevedore, and several "common laborers." Forty-four female patients were stated or inferred to be housewives by the use of the title "Mrs." In most of the female cases, social status could not be determined, although a few were described as "well-off," "wife of financier," or by some other term connoting social position. Seventeen patients, including several students, retirees, and dependents, and an asylum inmate, were classified as "other" since no information regarding class standing was given.

The case literature on neurasthenia illustrates physicians' perceptions of their nervous patients and brings to life the problems of real people. Statistical analyses drawn from the entirety of the case literature measure various aspects of the neurasthenic population but do not deal satisfactorily with the reality of abnormal mental conditions and the impact of such disabilities on the lives of patients and their families. A review of individual patient records combined with collective data on the entirety of the case literature provides insight into both the personal and the social dimensions of life in turn-of-the-century America. The evidence reveals clearly the universality of "nervousness" and related afflictions, both within the context of the nineteenth century and in comparison with contemporary society. While nineteenth-century Americans viewed the social problems of their age as unique, many of these same complaints are now seen as the exclusive product of twentieth-century life. The physical and psychosomatic symptoms experienced by individuals facing "life crises," diagnosed as neurasthenia a century ago, are today often characterized by the term *stress*—a word as nonspecific, unscientific, and loosely applied as *nervousness*. Though some of the conditions termed neurasthenia would today be classified as neuroses, while others—such as hypertension and ulcers—are recognized as stress-related but physical illnesses, the pathology of stress remains as elusive as ever. For this reason it is useful to examine the ways in which physicians perceived neurasthenia. Though nervous conditions were not "scientifically" understood and were frequently subjected to conflicting interpretations of causal relationship, physicians nevertheless believed that they were able to effect improvement in their patients' conditions. Since therapeutic success in the management of emotional disturbances depends in part on the confidence of health care providers in the particular methods employed, we have as much to learn from the nineteenth-century therapeutics of neurasthenia as from modern views on psychotherapy and stress management. The reading of individual cases, then, is instructive as well as interesting.

The symptoms observed in the case of Mr. W—— demonstrate the difficulty nineteenth-century physicians had in separating the significant from the trivial in cases of nervousness. Beard was particularly prone to exaggerating some symptoms at the expense of other, potentially more revealing ones; it was Mr. W——'s transient numbness of the extremities, in the case cited above, that particularly attracted his attention. His conclusion that Mr. W——'s illness was caused by overwork and "perhaps" excessive use of the sexual organs (though no evidence presented in the record justifies such an assumption) was likewise not uncommon. Recognizing mental causes of nervous conditions while employing physical remedies was likewise typical of Beard and of the 1870s, a decade in which he was the leading authority on neurasthenia. Beard treated Mr. W——, as was his custom, with electricity, which he supplemented with the internal administration of Horsford's acid phosphate, cod-liver oil, and counterirritation to the spine by means of "various blisters of cantharides and tartar-emetic ointment."[4]

This treatment continued for several months, and the patient gradually improved until he could attend to business "in a moderate way," slept better, and could walk farther. Thus, though Beard's analysis of Mr. W——'s case was rather perfunctory and was clearly influenced by preconceived notions, he treated Mr. W—— successfully, at least in his own opinion.

In the neurasthenic literature, the symptoms most commonly described by the patients reported on are consistent with physicians' beliefs that the illness could be detected by the presence of numerous subjective complaints and the absence of discoverable organic disturbance. Men and women complained equally of insomnia, indigestion or other gastric disturbance, depression, fears, muscular weakness, and heart palpitations. In addition, men were likely to complain of tingling or numbness of the extremities, lack of concentration, and sexual disturbances such as nocturnal emissions or prostration after coitus. Women frequently listed headache, generalized pains, loss of appetite, menstrual irregularity, ovarian pain, or amenorrhea (absence of the menses). A study of 333 clinic cases conducted by the New York City neurologist Joseph Collins and his clinical assistant Carlin Phillips, published in 1899, supports the journal literature evidence. Collins listed the most prominent symptoms of neurasthenia as insomnia, headache, depression, spinal weakness, indigestion, general pains, poor or variable appetite, constipation, heart palpitations, and nocturnal emissions.[5]

Although physicians disagreed as to which sex was more likely to suffer from neurasthenia, male and female patients were reported equally in the medical journal literature. Between 1870 and 1910 case reports of 154 men and 152 women were published in medical journals.[6] Most were probably married, though marital status was not reported in 137 cases and eight patients were widows.[7] The average male patient was thirty-seven and the average female thirty-five; 68 percent of the patients were between the ages of twenty-five and forty-five.

Patients described symptomatology easily recognized by modern readers as stress-related. A case related to the Boston Society for Medical Observation in 1872 by the alienist Theodore Fisher, for instance, records a woman whose primary symptom was "sick-headache," or in modern parlance, migraine. Mrs. B. was a thirty-year-old widow whom Fisher described as "always subject to sick-headaches, as was her mother before her . . . , of a nervous, sanguine temperament [though] in very good flesh and color. Menses regular in time, but excessive in quantity. Had several attacks of diarrhoea in summer of 1869, during a vacation in the country, and has felt weak and spiritless since her return. Is seldom constipated. Menstruated Nov. 1st, and has had headache since, with complete anorexia and occasional nausea."

"Find her in bed Nov. 6th, after a sleepless night," Fisher reported. "Complains of severe pain, confined, as usual, to a spot in left temple." Fisher prescribed valerianate of ammonia, and when the headache was relieved, an elixir of iron phosphate and strychnine. By November 9 Mrs. B was able to sit up, and Fisher directed her to take Angelica wine at luncheon and dinner. By November 21, he reported, "has improved in strength and appetite, but has headaches every few days. Now in bed from a cold, with headache. Sleeps badly. Pulse 76 and regular. Ordered potass. brom. grs. xv. at bedtime every night, and double the quantity when headache impends. Has tried chloral hydrate, with aggravation of pain, and will not take it again." As it did not prove effective, Fisher omitted the bromide and prescribed one-quarter grain of belladonna given daily instead.

By December Mrs. B. had successfully resumed her position as an instructress and bookkeeper in a sewing machine establishment. "The tendency to headache, with nausea, was inherited in this case," Fisher concluded. "It was also fostered by various sources of cerebral exhaustion in the individual, both recent and remote. The attacks occurred under such a variety of circumstances as to make it difficult to assign any special exciting cause." Thus, although Fisher recognized the role of mental strain ("cerebral exhaustion") in the attacks of "sick-headache," he confined himself primarily to treatment of the physical symptoms with specific remedies. He treated the "anorexia"—probably loss of appetite—by ordering a high protein diet, and added small amounts of rum and wine as relaxants and stimulants.[8] His treatments were typical of the therapeutics used by physicians of all specialties including alienists, neurologists, gynecologists, and general practitioners.

The case of Mrs. B. focused primarily on a pronounced physical symptom that could be treated specifically; in other patients the psychological or "mental" symptoms were more prominent. To these cases Beard's term *cerebrasthenia* was frequently applied, and physicians recognized that treatment of such patients must be directed toward the entire nervous system. In 1879 Beard described the case of a clergyman whom he diagnosed as a victim of "pure cerebrasthenia" or brain exhaustion:

> A gentleman of middle life, a clergyman by profession, had been engaged in labors of his calling in charge of a church under circumstances that drew severely on his patience and tact; about the same time he was prostrated by exposure to excessive heat, and the sequelae of this prostration were of a character quite frequently observed, namely a multitudinous array of nervous symptoms which annoyed him for a long time. These two factors together, acting on an inherited nervous diathesis, brought on a cerebrasthenia which, when I first saw the patient, had been present for a number of years, and had compelled him to change his ministerial position for that of teaching. He complained, first of all, of cerebral attacks, analogous to sick headache. . . . Other symptoms were indigestion, depression and at certain seasons, more or less diminution of sexual power. There was little or no trouble in the back, and no evidence of very great muscular debility; he could walk and work with the arms; all his symptoms pointed to the brain, especially these nervous attacks which, when they were upon him, unfitted him for any labor or enjoyment. They were excited by pulpit work, and, indeed by any form of mental annoyance, or by a feeling of responsibility; even the slight task of leading an evening prayer meeting or attending a funeral, was sufficient to induce an attack. . . . Iron alone was of little, if of any service, whereas he was certainly benefitted

by various electrical and medical treatment [*sic*] directed to the nervous system.[9]

Beard apparently missed the possibility that this former minister might not enjoy "pulpit work" as much as he felt he ought; the concept of the avoidance complex so well defined in post-Freud psychiatry texts was then unknown. Nevertheless, Beard introduced the case as one "especially interesting" because of the symptoms of agoraphobia, or fear of fears, that were so evident. (Beard apparently made a mistake in this case in stating that the patient had agoraphobia, which means fear of open spaces. He undoubtedly meant phobophobia.)[10] Recognition of the mental aspects of such symptoms led physicians to employ treatments like electrotherapy and strychnine, which had direct effects on the brain and central nervous system, and to devise programs intended to create more healthful mental attitudes. The mental framework was especially susceptible to influence when the symptoms appeared to be largely of a hysterical nature. It was for these patients, most often women, that the Mitchell rest cure treatment was devised.

Silas Weir Mitchell was among the most celebrated physicians of his time, and is said to have earned as much as $70,000 in a year.[11] His income derived from numerous consultantships in addition to his extensive private practice. His "rest cure" was devised primarily for fashionable ladies who could afford his high fees and were eager to receive his personal attentions. This treatment relied primarily on isolation of the patient, rest in bed, "passive exercise" such as massage, and full or even forced feeding. But Mitchell readily acknowledged that the success of his treatment depended largely on his own compelling personality and imperious manner. Some physicians criticized Mitchell as unscientific, if not actually unprofessional, but the rest cure grew in popularity throughout the period and was used in modified form by a wide variety of practitioners who attested to the fact that rest was in fact the best medicine for neurasthenics.

In 1879 the noted gynecologist William Goodell described a case in his presidential address to the annual meeting of the Ameri-

can Gynecological Society that testified to the efficacy of the rest
cure. Goodell reported the success he had had with the rest cure
"in those cases of back-ache and weariness and wakefulness which
tradition has labeled as disease of the womb, but which display no
coarse uterine lesions,—cases with leucorrhea [vaginal discharge],
or with amenorrhea, or with menorrhagia [heavy menstrual flow],
or with dysmenorrhea [painful menstruation], and yet so clad with
the livery of hysteria as to perplex alike the psychologist and
gynecologist." He recounted the following case to illustrate his
point:

> On March 6, of this year, a tall and large-framed girl of twenty
> was sent to me from a neighboring state. She was in wretched
> health and had been an invalid for some five years. Her cata-
> menia began at the age of thirteen and were for two years free
> from pain. Then, for some unexplained cause, dysmenorrhea
> began, which had gone on increasing until it was unbearable
> without anodynes. She suffered from aches all over her body,
> but more especially from back-ache and from constant and
> very severe pain on both ovarian regions, the left being the
> worse. She had frequent fits of unconsciousness (hystero-epi-
> lepsy), out of which she awakened with frightful screams. . . .
> To complete the category of ailments, she had leucorrhea, a
> uterine tenesmus [straining] which prevented her from walk-
> ing, obstinate costiveness [constipation], and a loss of all ap-
> petite. As her mother informed me, with probably some exag-
> geration, not a week had passed by for five years without
> several visits from her physician. . . . Feeling satisfied both
> from her history and from . . . examination that the dys-
> menorrhea was partly congestive . . . [but] that the severity of
> the symptoms was out of all proportion to the local lesions, I
> advised Mitchell's treatment.[12]

The patient spent forty-five days on the third story of her aunt's
home, to whose care she was consigned, and during this time saw
no one but the nurse who attended her daily, "the woman who
rubbed her," a Dr. George S. Gerhard, who administered electro-

therapy, and Goodell himself. The aunt was allowed brief daily visits later in the treatment. The patient was not allowed to read or write and was initially restricted to a skimmed milk diet. By the end of treatment, however, she had drunk 208 quarts of milk, consumed large quantities of eggs, and gained twenty-two pounds. She was discharged as cured and later wrote to Goodell: "I have been perfectly well ever since my return. I have walked with father two miles every evening, once over three miles; and, when I first saw you, could not walk across the room without screaming with the pain."[13]

Although hysterical forms of neurasthenia, like hysteria itself, were most often associated with women, men too were susceptible to the phobias that were recognized as hysterical reactions. Such obsessions or "fixed ideas" were frightening to patients and were important signs of neurasthenia. A clinic case demonstrated by the independent neurologist L. Harrison Mettler of Chicago in 1905 illustrates the pronounced mental symptoms of some neurasthenics:

> The next patient, B. Van D., aged seventeen, illustrates well a psychic state that we not infrequently see accompanying hystero-neurasthenia. The patient is a tailor by occupation and spends long hours in a confined position in an unhygienic workshop. His heredity is not bad, but it indicates a slight neuropathic condition in the family. He is nervous and physically much run down. There is insomnia, headache, vertigo, anorexia, constipation, alternate cold and hot sensations—in a word all the symptoms of a neurasthenic condition to a considerable degree. As you see he is thin and looks anaemic. His glance is furtive and he trembles readily. He complains of bad dreams and feels all the time a kind of dread.
>
> What he consults us primarily about, however, is his mental state in relation to the loss of a brother by drowning last year. He says that soon after his brother was drawn out of the water, dead, he saw him, and ever since then the shock has left him with a most horrible dread of water. He has an indistinct feeling, coupled with a tremendous fear, that some day he also will die by drowning. Hence for a whole year he has shunned

all forms of water, not even venturing to cross it on a broad and safe bridge. Sometimes his friends have inveigled him into approaching the river, but as soon as he has caught sight of the water he has fled precipitately back to his room, undergone violent trembling and in fear locked himself in for several days.

Mettler diagnosed the case as one of "phrenasthenia," a term that by the turn of the century had become synonymous with cerebrasthenia, and declared that the patient was a victim of "potamophobia" [fear of rivers and streams], "the result of a heightened degree of suggestibility . . . coupled with a weakening of the higher inhibitory reasoning faculty." Because such states were mild forms of psychosis and "not far removed from the hysterical state," Mettler observed, the treatment must be "along both psychic and materialistic lines." While the body must be built up with "good food, plenty of rest, and appropriate tonics . . . , the mental equilibrium must be restored by psychic suggestion steadily and frequently applied."[14] Mettler's approach exemplifies not only the diagnostic usefulness of neurasthenia as a classification for psychological and psychosomatic symptoms but also the integration of mental and physical treatments that pre-Freudian physicians viewed as essential to patient care. Concern with physical as well as emotional health resulted in improved "tone" and demonstrated that the doctor was truly interested in the patient's well-being.

Of course, no amount of concern shown by the physician could cure patients convinced of their imminent demise despite trivial symptoms. Such patients were obviously hypochondriacs, but when this tendency combined with a neuropathic diathesis, chronic nervousness was sure to be the result. Dr. E. C. Kinney, president of the Connecticut Medical Society in 1885, chose nervousness as the topic for his presidential address at the state society's annual meeting. He thought the subject appropriate because "in every day life there is no word more common with us, and perhaps none more difficult to define." New Englanders were "the most nervous people on the face of the earth," according to Kinney. "We have been living fast for a quarter of a century. All medical men who have given the subject any attention testify to the rapid and universal increase of nervousness." While Kinney thought most of the ills complained of by neurasthenics imaginary, the nervousness itself was real, resulting from "heredity, school pressure, and worry," among other causes. He cited the case of Miss ———, an "elderly lady on the shady side of forty," upon whom he had called as a young doctor soon after opening his practice, whom he described as "tall, angular, sharp-featured, with critical black eyes, and a strikingly nervous temperament."

First of all my patient informed me that she had been obliged to make a personal study of her own case. She had in her possession two family doctor books. She dilated on the respective merits of each. She was a subscriber to a health journal, and had the reading of a religious paper which devoted a column a week to hygiene. With this introduction she hoped I had leisure to hear a full account of her case. You may imagine it was a full account, for she detained me for an hour and forty minutes. A German professor on symptomology could not have given more symptoms, in a full hours' [*sic*] lecture.

She went from the hot place on the top of her head, to the cold ankles and the neuralgic pains in her great toe. There was no organ that escaped her notice. She had scattering pains that went galloping around like a flying artillery on a skirmish. She attached as many adjectives to her nouns as ever Rufus Choate did in his longest sentences. They were excruciating, tormenting, distressing, and all that. At last she came to a sudden halt, took a deep inspiration, looked me square in the face and as I had feared asked "Now what do you think my complaint is?" Having anticipated the question I was prepared to reply, "Madam, you are *overdone*." My patient had informed me during the interview that she had just dismissed a dress-maker, who had been in the house for two weeks. Whenever a nervous woman confesses that she has dismissed a dress-maker or a kitchen-servant, it is always wise to tell her she is overdone. In this instance the diagnosis was a success, it was eminently to the lady's satisfaction, "that was what she thought." In my experience no diagnosis is so comforting to a nervous woman as the assurance that she is *overdone*. It is as soothing as a poultice to a carbuncle.[15]

Finding that "no amount of reasoning" could reduce the number of Miss ———'s complaints, Kinney indulged this patient in her delusions and reported that she died of natural causes many years later, still surrounded by her pills and tonics. But though the tone of his address was lighthearted, Kinney and other physicians were aware that the difference between nervousness and insanity was but a question of degree; the apparently increasing numbers of neurasthenics were a source of concern to them. Kinney noted that in approximately 40 percent of the institutionalized cases of insanity he had observed, the cause of mental illness was unknown. These patients were not born insane, he claimed, "but like Topsy they grow insane." While the processes by which this occurred were as yet unknown, Kinney believed that "this form of insanity is largely due to nervousness, and is one phase of it. A great portion of our nervous patients are not insane, though they vibrate very close to insanity at times, and in paroxysms of high excitement bear a close resemblance to lunatics."[16]

While Kinney's Miss ——— was the victim of a harmless neurotic delusion, a few patients diagnosed as neurasthenic suffered from more serious mental disturbance. Arthur Conklin Brush, one of the most distinguished independent neurologist/alienist practitioners, described a case to the New York Medico-Legal Society in April of 1897 which he termed "cerebral neurasthenia" but which suggested a deeper mental derangement:

F. V. G., male. Mother very nervous. Sister now in an asylum. His friends have always considered him eccentric and unable to hold a connected conversation. He is fond of collecting useless objects, such as discarded bridge tickets. He keeps a large amount of very small bank accounts. He once killed a pet dog by pouring boiling water over its head; earns his living as an expert accountant. The first time he met his wife he asked her to marry him, and on refusal he produced a bible and read passages to prove to her that it was her duty to do so and also recited a prayer. This he repeated on subsequent visits, until she consented. During their engagement he constantly talked to her about the famous Baccaratt scandal of which she knew nothing. He was intensely jealous, even stealing her tennis racket to prevent her playing with other men. He would often leave her for long periods, even going to Europe, without communicating with her. During one of these absences he was arrested on the Brooklyn Bridge and committed to the Shepard Asylum, Baltimore, as an acute maniac. This was concealed from her. She broke the engagement but he continued to write to her incoherent, absurd and errotic [*sic*] letters, often sending them unsealed or on postal cards. She paid no attention to them. One day he forced his way into the house saying that her silence gave consent and that he had made all the arrangements for their wedding. He did not appear at the hour set but came some hours later, and they were married. He offered no explanation for this action. I will state that the reason she married him was as stated by a witness to me, that she was poor and her family thought him well off. After marrying he spent his nights in singing, dancing about the room, reciting poetry and often forcing his wife to take nocturnal walks with him in Prospect Park. He compelled her to wait on him, even to cutting up his food. His libido was intense and perverted, showing evidence of Saidism [*sic*], and he was also fond of doing disgusting and obscene things. He frequently tied his wife to a trunk and beat her, and he once kept her in an open boat for six hours, threatening to kill her. He frequently told her that a wife was entirely a man's property, and that he had a right to kill her. During her confinement he refused to obtain food, drugs or attendance, dragged her from the bed, knelt on her chest and prayed. She left him, but was induced to return. He then locked her in a room, telling her that he intended to kill her as he did the dog, which he considered a painless method. He frequently knelt on her chest and prayed to prepare for the sacrifice. She was rescued by some neighbors. After her escape he, not knowing her address, daily sent the same kind of letters and postal cards intended for her to her lawyer.

When served with the notice of the suit, he tore it up. He then discharged the lawyer, saying that he would defend the suit himself; but did not appear during the trial. After the trial he made frequent midnight calls on both her laywer and the medical expert.

Of the latter he demanded how he dared to testify against him; said he was not represented because he did not think any court would consider such a case; that he loved his wife and had provided a good home for her and was astounded that the decree had been granted. When subsequently arrested he acted in a perfectly rational manner.[17]

Probably most late nineteenth-century neurologists would have diagnosed F. V. G.—whose actions clearly indicated psychosis—as insane. But Brush, because of his training in traditional alienist theory, maintained that such patients differed from cases of true insanity because their symptoms were not "clear and well marked but run a chronic, ill-defined and often intermittent course." Though Brush felt that rehabilitation of such patients was practically impossible because of their degenerate neuropathic heredity, he found them "not insane enough for confinement, except for a time during a period of maniacal excitement" (a distinction, not incidentally, still evident in sanity hearings today). For such patients, fear of punishment was often an insufficient deterrent to crime, and though they might know the difference between right and wrong, they did not have the requisite judgment to apply their knowledge. Still, because, "as a rule there can be no question that they appreciate the consequences of their acts," Brush applied the M'Naghten rule of law that had swayed the Guiteau jury and classified F. V. G. as a victim of cerebral neurasthenia.[18]

The preceding illustrations provide a framework for understanding the range of conditions which physicians might diagnose as neurasthenia. While some patients were close to if not over the brink of insanity, most were victims of phobias, depression, or emotional stress. They were dangerous to no one except themselves, if suicidal, and their physical health was often good. Nevertheless, the suffering of such patients was very real, and physicians felt that some form of treatment was not only necessary but often effective in preventing permanent emotional illness.

After the turn of the century the optimism of mental hygienists was increasingly evident in the medical literature on neurasthenia. Many physicians believed that early intervention in cases of nervous degeneration could often restore patients and prevent development of true psychosis. Though patients with pronounced mental symptoms could be trying, they could often be saved from asylums if physicians recognized the dangerous ground on which they stood and implemented an early treatment program that incorporated mental as well as physical remedies. Charles W. Hitchcock, an independent neurologist from Detroit, read a paper entitled "Border Line Cases of Neurasthenia" before the Section on Medicine of the Michigan State Medical Society at its annual meeting in May of 1906. Hitchcock narrowed his attention to "the psychopathic side of its manifestations," noting a growing trend toward emphasis on "the psychic rather than the somatic symptoms." The purpose of his lecture was to encourage physicians to take appropriate action when such cases came under their observation. Because he believed patients of neuropathic heredity especially susceptible to insanity, Hitchcock emphasized the importance of taking a full history of every neurasthenic case and of inquiring particularly into family nervous background, a habit "too often neglected in general practice."[19]

Medical opinion was in fact divided over whether nervous conditions might be precursors to more serious mental illness, but physicians uniformly stressed the necessity of obtaining full histories from nervous patients. As the prominent Chicago neurologist Hugh Patrick remarked in discussing the case of a patient who suffered from nervous tingling of the extremities: "it is nothing dangerous; it is not a precursor of paralysis of any kind; it is not a precursor of insanity, nor is it the first step of any form of organic disease." Nevertheless, Patrick noted that the man's mother was insane, that he, two sisters, and his grandmother were all subject to migraine and that therefore the patient was "bound to be a neuropath." "We cannot remove a man's heredity," Patrick concluded, "but we may combat it by removing his anxiety and apprehension as much as possible, putting him on general tonics and good hygiene (especially cold baths), and recommending out-door exercise which is entertaining, amusing, and interesting."[20]

While physicians simply recorded symptoms as patients described them, they had more difficulty in assigning relative weight to causative factors. Heredity was clearly a significant element in the neurasthenic equation, but so too were environmental conditions. Given the theoretical importance physicians placed on discovering the nervous heredity of their patients, it is surprising that most of the case records published in medical journals failed to note such information; family history was reported in only 24 percent of the cases. Physicians may have assumed that the influence of heredity on nervousness was so well known that mention was unnecessary, or in practice they may have believed heredity less important in noninsane cases, contrary to their theoretical views. Certainly they were optimistic that even patients of decidedly nervous inheritance could learn to function more effectively. Of the cases in which family history was given, 52 percent of the male patients and 66 percent of the female patients were found to have had a nervous inheritance. The higher incidence of nervous heredity discovered in women was undoubtedly due to physicians' common belief that women were biologically predisposed to nervousness. Thus men became neurasthenic because of the external pressures of civilization; women, more sheltered from the world, were nevertheless prone to nervousness because they were inherently weaker.

While heredity accounted for predisposition to neurasthenia, any one of several well-known exciting causes could precipitate a nervous attack. Patients were diagnosed as suffering from peculiar forms of the disease depending upon the symptoms and underlying cause to which the attending physician attributed the illness. Thus a patient who had engaged in prolonged physical labor and complained of fatigue and backache was diagnosed as suffering from spinal neurasthenia; one with pronounced mental symptoms or who had devoted long hours to mental activity was a cerebrasthenic; and one who complained of gastric distress, indulged in the pleasures of civilized life, and took little or no exercise was pronounced a victim of lithemic (also lithaemic) or "assimilative" neurasthenia, otherwise known as "auto-intoxication." Among male cases reported in the journal literature, the most important exciting causes of nervous exhaustion were overwork or mental labor (32 percent), sexual excess (13 percent), anxiety (12 percent), ambition (10 percent), poisons like alcohol, tobacco, and drugs, and sedentary habits (7 percent each).

Because men normally led more varied lives than most women, involving themselves in career, family, and social activities both within and outside the domestic circle, physicians made greater distinctions in the causes to which they attributed male nervousness. Physicians also questioned men in more detail about their habits and personal affairs, partially because they were more likely to suspect men of hidden vice and partially because of the delicacy of raising intimate issues with members of the opposite sex. For a variety of reasons, then, articles dealing with the causes of neurasthenia in men are more varied and detailed—in short, more interesting—than those addressing the subject of cause in women. The following cases portray distinctions of cause among patients of both sexes and of varying social positions, but the female cases are cited following the male examples to illustrate differences in attributing cause of nervousness in women. Though an equal number of male and female patients were reported in the literature, fewer female cases are described here simply because the issue of causation was addressed in less detail for women than for men.

In an 1884 article on differential diagnosis, the Philadelphia neurologist Roberts Bartholow described a typical case of simple neurasthenia that resulted from overwork and mental fatigue, and that he termed the "anaemic" type:

Mr. ——, aged fifty-seven, lawyer by profession. He has immense mental energy, extraordinary quickness of perception, a capital logical and critical faculty, and fine oratorical power. These native abilities, conjoined with extensive cultivation, soon placed him amongst the foremost men at the bar of the city where he practiced, and have long maintained him in that position. . . . During the whole course of his professional life he has sustained no reverses, encountered no other anxieties than those of a successful lawyer, and has been rather singularly free, indeed, from the worries of life. Receiving, last summer, the nomination as a candidate to an important office, this cultivated gentleman, scholar, and lawyer, this man of nice tastes and high tone, entered on a canvass marked by vituperation and slander to an unusual extent. About the same time some business interests became entangled and caused no little worry. He began to have drenching night sweats, lost his appetite, grew weak, and was compelled to return home. It was then ascertained that he had malarial fever, and he was treated accordingly. But at this time and subsequently symptoms not necessarily of malarial origin appeared. . . . Every morning on awaking he was profoundly melancholic, and all the annoyances which the campaign had developed were gone over in his mind. He could talk of nothing else, think of nothing else than his ill feelings and the disagreeable political and personal slanders of which he had been made the victim. He complained much of the numbness of his hands, of weakness in the limbs, and he talked incessantly of his depressed feelings. . . . Presently . . . [he developed] insomnia, and he slept less and less, and rose in the morning haggard, exhausted, and horribly nervous and depressed. Ordinary hypnotics proved unequal to the effort to force sleep, and increasing doses of chloral became necessary. His mental activity, heretofore so remarkable, declined, and the effort to force his mind to the performance of any work, such as letter-writing, caused a sensation of fatigue. He also became undecided, even in small matters, ceased to have any inclination to go out and mingle with the public, and grew more and more averse to political movements. He reached a point finally when to meet strangers caused him great distress, excited the circulation, and induced a cold sweat.

As it became indispensable that he should resume the canvass he made a strong effort, and notwithstanding the fatigue, mental and moral depression, and exposure of public speaking, hand-shaking, and other matters of political expediency, he actually improved somewhat. . . . In a few weeks, by means chiefly hygienical, I succeeded in stopping the chloral; natural sleep was resumed, although it remained somewhat fitful. Suitable dietetic regulations, baths, exercise, and medicines . . . removed, or at least greatly modified, the principal symptoms. Two weeks at Atlantic City accomplished no little good, and when he returned to Philadelphia last week he appeared to be nearly his old self.[21]

Bartholow distinguished the "anaemic" (cerebral) form of neurasthenia displayed by Mr. ———— the attorney from what he called the "congestive" type typified by Mr. ————, a railroad executive. The latter case exemplified what was commonly called lithemic neurasthenia, a less prestigious form of the disease associated primarily with overindulgence in food and drink. It was described by Bartholow in the following account:

Mr. ————, aged forty-four, president of one of the largest railroad corporations of the West. Beginning his career at an early age in a subordinate position, he has, by the force of a superior intellect and of a physique that no labor could subdue, risen to the highest office, and now controls vast interests. Ambitious, enterprising, resolute, he has carried these faculties into all his work, and has shrunk from no tasks, however severe—from no responsibility, however onerous. As he has risen in position, social engagements have also added to his burdens. His habits have become more sedentary, . . . the pleasures of the table, including wine-drinking and late suppers, have been more and more indulged in; excessive smoking has been added to these indulgences; and thus, whilst his physical powers have been slowly impaired by bad hygiene, the demands on his mental powers have increased.

Three years ago Mr. ———— observed that he was not feeling well, and that he could not work as before. He became dull, especially after meals, had a constant headache, dizziness and throbbing of the temples; he applied his mind with difficulty, and all of the head symptoms were increased by the efforts made; he had a good, rather a keen appetite; a heavily coated tongue, flatulence, constipation, and some colic pains. The bladder was rather irritable, especially at night; sexual inclination had declined with lessened power, and various ill-defined but annoying sensations were felt about the penis, scrotum, and perinaeum. . . . Subjectively the following symptoms are experienced: Various strange sensations in the scalp; a persistent headache; blurred vision at times; vertiginous [whirling, dizzy] feelings occurring irregularly and of varying severity; despondency, vague apprehensions; fear of places, especially of crowded assemblages; difficulty of deciding questions very trivial or otherwise, in place of former promptness; impaired memory for persons, names, and things. Notwithstanding this extended list of symptoms Mr. ——— did not have an ill look, but, on the contrary, on superficial examination, appeared to be robust. To him and his immediate family the situation seemed in a high degree alarming. The surrender of his position and his business interests was regarded as imminent. To the apprehension awakened by his head symptoms was added the diagnosis of cerebral congestion, and hence the profound melancholy into which he was plunged.[22]

Bartholow thought the congestive type of neurasthenia not uncommon, "as Beard admits," though he acknowledged the anemic form as more prevalent. Physicians like A. D. Rockwell, Beard's former partner, were purists who wanted to restrict the diagnosis of neurasthenia to the sensitive, high-strung intellectual class for whom Beard intended the term. Rockwell took exception to the frequent diagnosis of lithemic neurasthenia in an article published in 1888. He complained that neurasthenia, "now almost a household word," was a convenient refuge for physicians faced with a perplexing array of unconnected symptoms and a pleasing diagnosis to patients who could proudly "allude to themselves as the victims of nervous exhaustion." Many of these patients were not neurasthenics, Rockwell declared scornfully, "and under hardly any conceivable circumstance could they become neurasthenic. They do not belong to the type out of which neurasthenia is born, either mentally or physically." Rockwell distinguished lithemia as a gastric disease that prevailed among the "unintellectual, phlegmatic, and intolerably indolent"; such patients, he believed, needed more mental and physical activity, not less. He first described a case illustrating what he termed neurasthenia "pure and simple":

> Mr. O., aged thirty-six, . . . Physically he was well developed, standing five feet ten inches in his stockings, and weighing 170 pounds. His complexion was fair, his eyes were blue, his hair was blonde, and his nutrition was apparently unimpaired. Intellectually he was far above the average. He could speak correctly two languages other than his own, besides understanding and writing a third, and all this he had mostly acquired through self-instruction. In addition to the labor necessitated by these scholastic acquirements, he had devoted himself for years, with few intervals of rest, to the details of an exacting mercantile business. . . . To this time he had not given up the general supervision of his business, but soon after coming under my observation he was induced to leave New York indefinitely. He journeyed to the West, visited the Yellowstone region, and at San Francisco took steamer for China. He was absent some eighteen months, and returned a well man, nor has he since relapsed into his former condition.[23]

Here indeed was a perfect specimen of the pristine nervous American, a credit to his country, his race, and his physician. Contrasting this picture with the less attractive lithemic patient, Rockwell described the case of Mr. N., "a stout gentleman with a somewhat sallow complexion." This patient, like Mr. O., complained chiefly of constipation and depression, but Rockwell snobbishly refused to diagnose him as neurasthenic and reported simply that the patient improved considerably under a change of diet and the institution of an exercise program.[24] Despite Rockwell's exclusivist diagnostic policy, many physicians continued to employ the term *lithemic neurasthenia,* and this form of nervousness accounted for a considerable number of cases, though it remained less important than the varieties resulting from mental labor and sexual excess.

The belief that masturbation led to mental illness was a tenet of Victorian society. Physicians railed at the shameless use of this theory by quack advertisers at the expense of young men who feared insanity, but they too thought "self-abuse" related to the development of mental disorders. Sexual neurasthenia was often the diagnosis when it was learned that the patient was or had been in youth a habitual masturbator; not surprisingly it was a common form of the disease in males. Both masturbation and sexual "excess" (as defined by the physician according to the merits of each case) were frequent causes of neurasthenia in males. Francis B. Bishop, an electrotherapist, reported a case of sexual neurasthenia to the November 1897 meeting of the Medical Society of the District of Columbia that illustrates the use physicians frequently made of the term. Bishop claimed that the case was "very interesting from the fact that his general mental condition was such that, *legally,* he would have been considered thoroughly responsible for his actions, for he was naturally an intelligent man and confided to no one but his physician the terrible obsessions that almost took possession of him, from time to time, in the form of a sudden impulse to kill his own child." As Bishop described the case:

A young gentleman of twenty-eight, presenting the appearance of one in fairly good health, addicted to masturbation in early youth, was married shortly before consulting me. He used tobacco freely, and gave a history of excessive indulgence in sexual intercourse. He complained of dizziness during the day, a twitching of muscles of the extremities at night, which would come on just as he was dropping off to sleep; he would awaken with the most violent palpitation of the heart. These conditions would frequently keep up during the better part of the night, almost exhausting the patient before morning, and rendering him quite useless for his daily work. By abstaining from his excesses, and by the use of galvanic, faradic, and static electricity, he soon recovered. Eighteen months later, he called upon me again, stating that since he had seen me, he had become the father of a baby boy, which was, at that time, about one year old. His old excesses gradually returned and with them, his old symptoms to an exaggerated degree. While sitting quietly in the midst of his little family, he would be suddenly impelled by a diabolical impulse, to murder his own little baby. The sight of a knife or any sharp instrument, would suggest the idea; then the morbid impulse would urge him to carry out the suggestion, and it was only by the most extraordinary exercise of the will, that he would force himself to leave the presence of the child to keep from yielding. There were no hallucinations in this case, nor delusions, but an impulse closely approaching those of insanity. His powers of reasoning and of the will were mercifully spared, and thus was averted the most horrible infanticide, followed perhaps, by suicide. Abstinence from excesses, and the use of tonics, baths and electricity completely restored this gentleman. A period of ten years has elapsed; there are several children in the family, and there has never been the slightest suspicion of a return of his trouble.[25]

While predisposition to nervousness was a fact of inheritance and thus to be pitied, exciting causes carried connotations of guilt or innocence. Not surprisingly, physicians tended to judge their nervous patients as "good" or "bad" depending on the cause to which they attributed the disease. Although not enough data for valid statistical analysis was available in the case literature, and judgmental descriptions are subject to varying interpretations, it is clear from the use of such terms as "hard-working" or "furtive" that physicians did form opinions of their patients' characters. Doctors did not usually praise or blame openly, probably out of respect for the confidentiality of the doctor-patient relationship (though this seems less true for clinic cases than for private patients), but casual remarks made elsewhere in the articles, in addition to occasional judgments made in case records, make possible some inferences regarding physicians' impressions of their patients' relative value to society.

Patients who were prostrated by overwork and anxiety were obviously blameless for their illnesses and even admirable for trying
to accomplish more than they reasonably could. Those whose condition resulted from dissipations—overindulgence in food, "poisons," or sexual activity—or from hereditary degeneration, were
less praiseworthy. As Hugh Patrick explained,

> there are, in my opinion, two distinct kinds of neurasthenia,
> which must be differentiated as regards both their nature and
> treatment. The first are the cases that are caused by an ade-
> quate influence,—that is, there is an adequate, reasonable
> cause for a certain result. In patients who overwork them-
> selves, who have had great loss of sleep and prolonged de-
> pressing emotions, the ordinary every-day cases of nervous ex-
> haustion, there has been an amply sufficient strain to exhaust
> the nervous system, consequently to produce true neuras-
> thenia. On the other hand, there are the distinctly neuropathic
> cases which fall into a similar condition from inadequate
> cause. They have not been subjected to prolonged depressing
> emotions, to over-mental work, to loss of sleep, and to worry
> and wear and tear of the nervous system, but they are the vic-
> tims of an idea, or conception, or other mental impression
> which goes on working and impressing again and again and
> gradually evolving certain nervous states. The cases of neur-
> asthenia which occur from slight traumatism, which develop
> after a slight illness, after a single mental shock or powerful
> emotion, are the distinctly neuropathic cases. In them there is
> an original neuropathic condition, nearly always inherited.[26]

The class biases of physicians are evident in their attribution of
causes of neurasthenia for different occupation groups. Doctors,
like most middle-class Americans, believed the upper classes to be
hardworking and ambitious while the lower classes were of grosser,
more animallike sensibilities, and their diagnoses reflected their
opinions. (An example of the ways in which physicians might in-
terpret similar symptomatology differently is found in the case of
sexual neurasthenia cited above. Interestingly, Bishop had reported

the same case to his medical society at a meeting six years earlier. What he neglected to mention in his second report was that at their first conference he had advised this young mechanic to live apart from his wife because of his habit of "having intercourse from one to three times every night since his [recent] marriage"; the urge to kill his child occurred after the patient was reunited with his wife and new baby.)[27] The most frequent causes of nervous exhaustion among male patients of the professional class were overwork or mental labor (34 percent); poisons and sedentary habits (14 percent); anxiety (13 percent); and sexual excess (12 percent). In men of the laboring class, by contrast, the most important causes were sexual excess (33 percent); trauma (20 percent); and overwork (13 percent).

Similar stereotypes typified physicians' views of women and influenced their beliefs about nervousness in the "weaker sex." The causes of neurasthenia most frequently reported for women were genital/reproductive disturbances, including exhaustion of childbirth (31 percent); trauma (16 percent); and overwork, anxiety, and other local disturbances (each reported in 10 percent of the cases). Causes listed less frequently included inappropriate behavior for her sex—such as attending college—boredom, heredity, and excesses. Women were diagnosed as suffering from overwork if, and only if, they were burdened with heavy and unavoidable responsibilities, "adequate cause" in Patrick's terminology. Since arduous duties usually devolved only on women of limited financial circumstances, instances of overwork in women were more commonly found among patients who could not afford servants. An example of this type of case was reported by Dr. Frank D. Bain of Kenton, Ohio, in 1897, who described it as

> the most desperate case of my observation—a female patient, 55 years of age, who nursed her mother through a protracted illness. So devoted was she to her aged parent that she gave every hour of the twenty-four to attendance at the bed-side; day after day and week after week she remained faithful in her vigils, when at last the fatal termination of the case occurred. The shock was too great and this devoted daughter found her-

self the victim of a complete nervous exhaustion. This case exhibited all the features of nervous collapse. Nearly three years have elapsed and this patient is far from regaining her accustomed health.[28]

The data on attribution of cause of nervousness to local disturbances in women must be used with caution because gynecologists reported 20 percent of the female cases; these specialists invariably assigned the highest priority to reproductive problems. But it is evident from the writings of neurologists, alienists, general practitioners, and other physicians that the regular medical profession generally believed woman's nervous system to be subordinate to her reproductive organs. Even physicians like Margaret Cleaves, one of only six female doctors to write on neurasthenia, found women particularly prone to nervousness and sometimes to enjoyment of their invalidism. Cleaves stated in a paper read at the annual medical association meeting in her home state of Iowa in 1886: "Women who have no attraction to take them from a subjective study of their ills, delight in their role of invalid and live 'upon the sweet counsel of their physician and the daily ministration of loving friends, and upon whom the house physician like the house fly is in chronic attendance.'"[29]

Cleaves was by no means unsympathetic to the problems that she felt produced neurasthenia among women, believing herself a victim. She thought that neurasthenia occurred most often in women of intelligence, education, and culture and sometimes in those of "well-balanced mental organizations." "In no country or time," she held, "has there been so much would-be mental activity among women as here and now. *True* mental activity should not result in injury but good, but carried on as the struggle is, to keep up with the demands of the times, to fulfill the duties of wives, mothers and homekeepers, with never ending social duties, and under unhygienic influences," it was no wonder that women succumbed as did the beautiful N. E. ("nervous exhaustionist") satirized by Augustus Hoppin in "A Fashionable Sufferer." "Women, more than men," Cleaves maintained, "are handicapped at the outset, not necessarily because they are women, but because, suddenly and without the previous preparation that men for generations have had, they attempt to fulfill certain conditions and are expected to qualify themselves for certain work and distinctions."[30] Cleaves believed herself a victim of such circumstances: in the book known to be her own autobiography, she described a woman whose mistress was science and whose patients were family and friends. She had tried to become her "father's boy" after the death of her only brother, but her father's death when she was fourteen deprived Cleaves of the guardian whom she believed would have protected her in later life. Though she found in New York a physician—her "professional confessor"—whose sympathy provided human contact in what otherwise must have been a lonely existence, it was only by the careful regulation of her life that Cleaves found herself able to live within her slender nervous endowment.

It was their biological nervous weakness, physicians believed, that made women particularly prone to acute attacks of nervous exhaustion following emotional shocks. The unexpected arrival of disturbing news such as a lover's defection was the frequent cause of prostration among heroines of romantic novels; physicians reported that survivors of natural disasters and tragic accidents were just as likely to succumb in the aftermath of emotional trauma. Women were the most common victims of traumatic breakdowns because of their generally nervous and excitable nature. Beard, for example, described a typical case of traumatic neurasthenia that resulted from the sinking of the steamship Seawanaka:

I have now under my care a lady who was one of those on board at the time, and with her family was saved, but who has never been well from that day to the present. She was not in perfect health before, but all her evil symptoms are much aggravated by the accident. The steamer was rapidly burned, but she used a life-preserver, jumped over and was saved, after being a long time in the water, but the excitement of the accident, the anxiety with regard to her family brought on a reaction which appears in the following symptoms: mental depression, a movement of the head from side to side on retiring, nervous cough, stiffness of the neck at times with symptoms of

spinal irritation, podalgia, swelling of the feet, and so remarkable is the influence of the mind, that any trouble causes pain
in the feet; poor appetite, poor digestion, very poor and uncertain memory. This patient has also a morbid fear, she is
afraid to go to the theatre especially, because she apprehends
that if a fire breaks out she cannot escape, and yet at the opera
she is not in trouble. Even now, after she has improved very
decidedly in all her symptoms, she does not think she can ven-
ture to the theatre. Another illustration of very many that the
morbid fears are the hardest symptoms to cure, among the
neurasthenics. She also fears sound, noises of any kind, and
when I began to treat her, she could not bear the sound of the
farradic [*sic*] battery, and I was compelled to use the galvanic,
since electricity was one of the various remedies which I
wished to use in her case. . . . This lady is a person of strong
will and decision, and not disposed to magnify, but rather to
minify [*sic*] her troubles, and was induced to take treatment
through her husband's persuasion rather than her own will.
The case is of interest, as illustrating the well-known law that
though one may be cool in the hour of peril, and have great
presence of mind, yet, all must be paid for in nerve force, and
if one be poor in nerve force, the account is overdrawn by
these excitements, and it may take some months and some
times years to recuperate. . . . I have seen illustrations of the
fact, that, after great fires and accidents of any kind where
men are injured, there is still a large number whose nervous
systems are injured, but whose names do not appear in the
papers, and who are never reported as sufferers, but who do
suffer in the way above described, far more, perhaps, in some
instances, than those who have broken limbs or disfigured
countenances.[31]

Physicians of different specialties debated whether the spinal
tenderness and ovarian pains characterized as "congestion" and
commonly complained of by female neurasthenics were organic or
mental in origin, with neurologists and some gynecologists taking
opposing sides of the argument. Most doctors took the middle

ground on this question, recognizing two classes of neurasthenia: those in which local disease caused the nervous condition, and those in which local manifestations were the result of it. More moderate gynecologists usually held this view and explicitly described the care they took in determining the true cause of each case. As Edward Reynolds, a gynecologist, wrote of the ongoing debate between surgeons and neurologists in 1910: "The truth probably lies midway between the failure of many surgical specialists to realize the presence and sometimes the dominating importance of neurasthenia in their cases; and, on the other hand, the equally grave failure of many neurologists and general practitioners to realize the presence and at least contributing importance of local lesions in the same cases. In fact," he claimed, "both elements are present in varying degrees of importance in most (but not all) neurasthenias."[32]

Frederick Coggeshall, a gynecological surgeon in the Department of Nervous Diseases at the Boston Dispensary, chose "The Relation of Local Disease to Nervous Disorders, Especially Neurasthenia" as his address to the Boston Society for Medical Improvement in November 1901. Coggeshall found the growing trend toward specialization in medical practice a mixed blessing and blamed many incomplete and mistaken diagnoses on the increasing narrowness of medical practice. "Divergence of opinion upon such a subject is the natural consequence of the tendency to such early and complete specialization in practice," he declared, "which, with all its admirable results in the mastery of technique and in completeness of knowledge along one line, must, save in exceptionally broad-minded men, result in a strange incompleteness of knowledge of human beings as a whole."[33] Coggeshall drew attention to the necessity of considering both local disturbances and mental states in treating nervous patients. He illustrated the sometimes beneficial effect of surgery on disturbed women with the following case:

Mrs. B., apparently a very healthy, well-nourished woman twenty-one years of age, consulted me in the Boston Dispensary for what she called "nervousness." She complained of severe pain in the sacrum and right iliac region, insomnia, and entire lack of control over her emotions, so that she would cry upon the slightest provocation, or without any at all. There was also excessive sexual appetite for the last two years. Menstruation had begun at fourteen, with severe pain in the left iliac region at every period.

A sclerocystic ovary was removed by Dr. Ernest Cushing from the left side when she was fifteen; this gave complete relief to her dysmenorrhoea. She married at eighteen, had a healthy child at nineteen, and for a year after continued to enjoy good health.

For the past year the symptoms of which she now complained had been increasing in severity. Some two months ago she consulted a woman physician, who sent her into the hospital for observation and treatment. There she remained for six weeks, being frequently examined by a number of different doctors. During this time she became more and more hysterical and excitable, and the doctors were unwilling to operate because she was in such a nervous state, and finally discharged her because she became so unmanageable, and referred her to the mental department of the Boston Dispensary. Acting upon her physician's assurance that there was no local cause for her complaints of pain, and upon her obviously unbalanced condition, the eminent alienist who saw her advised her commitment to an asylum, which was to have taken place within a day or two of the time I first saw her. I referred her to the gynaecological clinic, of which I was in charge at that time, and found upon examination a beautifully healed abdominal scar, the result of Dr. Cushing's operation. The tube and ovary on the left side could not be found. The right ovary was prolapsed, enlarged, and exquisitely sensitive. The uterus, three inches and one fourth deep, was retroflexed, and the fundus firmly adherent in the hollow of the sacrum.

I sent her into the hospital at once and operated forty-eight hours later. I very reluctantly removed the whole of the remaining ovary, as it was impossible to find a trace of normal tissue in it. The uterus was curetted, its adhesions broken up, and fastened in place by a ventral suspension. The patient made a perfect recovery and regained her mental balance to a great extent, but suffered severely from hot flushes for the next eight months, when she developed a gastric ulcer, for which I sent her into the Massachusetts Hospital, in the service of Dr. Vickery. She made a good recovery, but meanwhile her husband had acquired gonorrhoea and infected her soon after her return. She had had a slight return of her nervous symptoms during her stomach trouble, and when she developed a severe gonorrhoeal endometritis they came back again with many hysterical symptoms. Treatment was neglected and infection was so severe that she was again sent to the hospital. The surgeon under whose care she came felt justified in doing a vaginal hysterectomy, on the ground that the uterus was useless to her and that it was greatly diseased. She again made a good recovery from the operation and all her nervous and mental symptoms disappeared. In the course of the next few months, however, she had an abscess in the external auditory canal and another in her lip. Both were, of course, extremely painful. With each, the nervous symptoms returned, to disappear as soon as the pain was relieved.

Coggeshall concluded his report by noting that "for the past two years and a half nothing new has happened to her and she has been earning her living as a waitress and has enjoyed excellent health except for occasional headaches."[34]

Coggeshall sincerely believed that his patient's nervousness was relieved by the succession of operations performed on her reproductive organs. Other physicians reported the successful treatment of nervousness in women by ovariotomies, hysterectomies, and surgical repair of perineal lacerations. (Equivalent procedures, especially the introduction of sounds to enlarge urethral stricture, were performed on males, though with far less frequency—and, of course, with less permanent physical effects.) The perception that mental health depended on the healthy integration of individual

parts was a distinctly holistic nineteenth-century view. Given the
well-established belief that woman's biology dictated an interrela-
tionship between her mind and her reproductive system, the emphasis on female surgery for nervous conditions was predictable.
Most of these patients were, in fact, "nervous"; they were not unwilling guinea pigs but sufferers who sought relief. If doctor and
patient shared faith in a particular remedy—be it surgery, drugs,
or applications of electricity—the patient was often truly benefited,
though relief may have been temporary. Anticipating the charge
that surgical treatment of neurasthenia had no permanent value,
physicians commonly reported that follow-ups found former patients well and attending to their affairs two, three, or more years
later, though, of course, their claims cannot now be validated.

The belief that women were less well "nervously prepared" than
men affected both women's responses to stress and physicians' perceptions of nervousness in male and female patients. As Cleaves
observed, some women enjoyed their status as the weaker sex and
used their positions as invalids to their best advantage. At the same
time, physicians' views that nervousness was more "natural" in
women led them to see the disease as less severe in female patients.
While 56 percent of the neurasthenic women reported on in medical journals were described in terms suggesting extreme nervousness, only 18 percent were characterized as being close to insanity.
(Twenty-six percent were described as mild cases.) Among male
patients, 29 percent were "mildly nervous," and 32 percent "very
nervous," but a large number—39 percent—were found to be on
the "borderland" of insanity. Although male and female cases were
equally represented in the literature, then, men who displayed pronounced nervous symptoms were more than twice as likely to be
declared close to insanity.

The case literature on neurasthenia makes clear that physicians
saw differences in the origin of nervousness in men and women,
though the symptoms were virtually identical. Except for surgery,
treatments too were much the same for male and female patients,
but physicians had more success in treating female neurasthenics.
Perhaps because of women's greater tractability and physicians'

Table 2. Treatment Outcome

	Men	Women
Cured	18 percent	24 percent
Some or Much Improved	49	51
Worse or Stopped Treatment	9	11
No Report	24	14
	100	100

perceptions that some nervousness was acceptable in the female sex, women were more likely to be pronounced cured or improved. Twenty-four percent of the female patients were reported "cured" and 51 percent some or much improved; 11 percent were found to be in the same or worse condition or to have stopped treatment, and no outcome was reported in 14 percent. Among male patients, 18 percent were declared cured and 49 percent some or much improved; 9 percent were the same, worse, or had stopped treatment, while the outcome of 24 percent of the cases was not reported. The greater percent of unreported outcomes for treatment of males suggests that men were less likely than women to make either partial or complete recoveries from nervous exhaustion (hence physicians' reluctance to report outcomes). As with differences between the sexes in the severity of the disease, physicians may have had a more narrow view of accepted male behavior and thus regarded evidence of nervous weakness in men as abnormal.

Throughout the years from 1870 to 1910, physicians of all types displayed increasing recognition that psychological treatment alone could have just as great an effect on neurasthenic patients as physical remedies. This was not so much a revolutionary idea as an extension of the long-known fact that physical treatments were often of more use for their psychic value than for any physical effect. Surgery and other drastic measures declined as physicians reported success in treating nervousness almost entirely by mental methods. Resourceful doctors relied on imaginative forms of "suggestion," usually without the patient's knowledge, to persuade sufferers that their conditions were improving and that good health would ultimately be theirs. The forms of mental treatment used were sometimes crude, but physicians felt their methods justified if they stopped the inroads being made on the regular medical profession by Christian Scientists and other "mind curists." Dr. Joseph L. Bauer of St. Louis, for example, demonstrated his successful psychological treatment of several nervous patients in a paper read before the Bond County [Illinois] Medical Society in 1894. The simple techniques that he employed, he declared, were "not the property alone of exceptional (hypnotists, Christian science, faith curists, etc.) individuals," but were "within the power of every physician of ordinary capabilities and individuality." Moreover, Bauer asserted, he would show how the bromides, "that favorite nostrum, of most uncertain efficacy," could be relegated "to the apothecary's shelves" where they belonged. To prove his claim, Bauer cited the following case:

> Seven years ago, I was asked to see Mrs. G., aet 42, a fat woman of small stature, who had not walked for twelve years. . . . Upon visiting her I found a well preserved German woman with pale face and flabby musculature, presenting no evidence whatever of ill health or nerve impairment, except the fixed idea that she could not walk. Her meals were regularly supplied in bed, and nature's demands assisted by the use of a bed pan. All her motions were perfect whilst in a recumbent or "I cannot; if I do, I will die!" sitting posture, but every effort toward influencing her to walk was negatived by the response.
>
> It may seem presumptuous to state that when asked if I could cure her, I answered affirmatively, without any reservation, excepting that I insisted upon her removal to my vicinity away from accustomed influences. It was difficult to secure consent to this request, but after arranging a mattress upon a spring wagon, and handling her as gently as a dainty piece of bric a brac, we succeeded in overcoming all obstacles. My positive conviction that she could be relieved of this peculiar ailment . . . rested upon the principle that her apprehension had grown to a habit or fixed idea, a condition not unusual

amongst intelligent people, and very common among the ignorant. And by creating another and more potent dominant or fixed idea, I could dethrone this monomaniacal vagary and supplant it by another of greater intensity for a sufficient length of time to permit the return of the self-assertion she so much needed.

[Bauer described how his patient] was placed in a comfortable bed and allowed to rest until the next morning, when my treatment was to begin. This was initiated without any preliminaries. I presented a small bottle of medicine, in which a camel's hair pencil was placed. I stated succinctly and positively that her ailment depended upon some difficulty in the middle third of each thigh, and the medicine was for the purpose of restoring power. Further, I enlarged upon its great, though alarming potency, necessitating immediate locomotion lest death instantly follow our failure to observe precautions. A small quantity was suggested as primarily required and five minutes locomotion a necessary requisite. No difficulty followed the suggestion, and our patient walked with her physician during the allotted time. This was kept up for two weeks, a larger quantity of painting each day and an increase of the time limit. Upon the termination of this period she walked six miles without objection or fatigue. I considered her relieved and sent her home, admonishing her not to forget the daily painting of our mixture. Having heard excellent reports of her continued welfare, it was thought best to overcome the new formed habit. This was done by a careful examination of her limbs, and a sudden, forceful and jubilant exclamation that the two spots had recovered completely. To give her a further practical demonstration of the fact, she was advised to attend a dance which she greatly enjoyed.[35]

Bauer was justifiably proud of his successful treatment of the case and was not disturbed that the method employed was identical to those well known among purveyors of patent medicines. Though physicians spoke out loudly and often against the harm done by quack advertisers, they believed the same remedies could be used to good effect by their own profession. Physicians more scrupulous than Bauer addressed the topic hesitantly, but with the conviction that failure to treat nervous patients left the sufferers prey to the despised Christian Scientists and other nonmedical healers. John P. C. Foster, in "Suggestive and Hypnotic Treatment of Neurasthenia," a paper read before the New Haven County Medical Association in April 1901, acknowledged his reluctance to speak on the subject: "Even at the present time—after years of absolute demonstration of its value—I find myself hesitating to write of suggestion and hypnotism as therapeutic agents." But, said Foster, investigations over the past twenty years had proven suggestion, with or without hypnotism, to be of scientific value and asserted that "more can be accomplished by mental sugges- tion in neurasthenia than by all the drugs in the materia medica."[36] By way of example Foster cited the case of "a lady who was in New Haven to educate her sons":

> She was a thin, care-worn, anxious neurasthenic. She was pos- sessed of large wealth and was continually seeking the advice of the most eminent men in medicine in this country. A great medical name seemed to charm her, and she invariably re- turned to New Haven with a diagnosis of serious import from each and every specialist. I wish I could with propriety men- tion some of her medical advisers by name. She finally re- turned to town with an undoubted malignant tumor in her abdomen. She had accepted the decree and declined an opera- tion. She was calmly preparing to die. I never could discover any of her maladies, nor even the cancer; but I was merely her medical man in a small way and could gain no control over her imagination, because of the preeminence of her New York and Philadelphia advisers. When her son was graduated she left town. To die? No; to become a Christian Scientist in Boston; to actually visit that Eddy woman herself.[37]

"That case goes down in history as a cancer cured by Mrs. Eddy," pronounced Foster disgustedly. He urged physicians not to humor or ignore nervous patients carried away by their imaginations but to resort to whatever means necessary to cure patients of their real trouble. "May the day come and come quickly," he pleaded,

> when the medical man will not regard his profession as the giving of drugs, but will dare, when drugs fail, to use any and every agency to secure the relief for which his patient has sought his advice. Our profession is to relieve the sick and se-cure, if possible, a return to health. As one reads medical literature of the better sort nowadays, it sometimes seems as if the only real interest was in a diagnosis and an autopsy; but the public do not look at the matter in that way, and they will seek relief where it can be found. Can we not let them see that we use all that there is of good in any real cure, and teach them the utter folly of all else in Eddyism and such like? [38]

Many physicians reported that they used suggestion to a greater or lesser extent in their practices and testified to its positive effect. But suggestion was only one of several mental techniques that phy-sicians termed "education of the patient" and that played an im-portant role in therapeutics throughout the neurasthenia years. Treatment programs, involving thorough examination of the pa-tient with complete family history, appropriate medicinals, and various psychological measures, were described by physicians from the late 1870s into the early twentieth century. These were usually not miracle cures or overnight successes like that described by Bauer but lengthy therapies requiring tact, patience, judgment, and true sympathy for the patient's condition. There was no writ-ten formula for application, but the lack of system placed the em-phasis of treatment exactly where physicians though it should be—that is, on the needs of the individual patient. Because there were no formulas for success, each case was a challenge requiring careful analysis and close supervision. Two cases described by Dr. Charles D. Center of Quincy, Illinois, in a 1904 paper entitled "The Educational Treatment of Neurasthenia," demonstrate the varia-tions in treatment which a physician might employ depending on the facts of the case:

Male, age 46. Confirmed neurasthenic for ten years. His mother is a neurasthenic. One brother and one sister are neurasthenics, and he has a neurasthenic daughter. His neurasthenia followed a period of excessive work, very unusual mental strain, and considerable forced loss of sleep. This patient's obsession was a fear of being alone, and of becoming over heated. For ten years he had not gone from his house to his office alone. He had practically lived out doors in winter and in his cellar in the summer to avoid becoming over heated. After two weeks spent with intestinal eliminants, and an every other day interview to gain his confidence, he was given the syrup of the iodide of iron for a moderate degree of anemia, and instructions to drive his horse from his house to his office with a member of the family walking on the sidewalk beside him. After the third day the attendant walked one-half block behind him, and in another week the attendant was dispensed with. He now, at the end of six months, goes about alone and is the picture of health and contentment. His fear of heat was overcome partly by his being told that his tonic would cool his blood, partly by his own regained self control.[39]

Center's next case involved a patient who was severely depressed and suicidal. The treatment prescribed met turn-of-the-century requirements for individualization, if nothing else. The unusual approach was apparently effective in this case, at least in Center's view:

Male, age 39. Bookkeeper. Case developed gradually. Supposed excess in this case, too close application to ledger. Chief obsession, the fear of killing himself, or some member of his family. He could not read the papers because he saw nothing in them but suicide, murder and sudden death. His insomnia was grave. He was given for three weeks sufficient bromide during the early evening to make him sleep. Also a digestive mixture. He was instructed to lie down for one hour in the middle of the day, to walk instead of taking the street cars, and whenever he contemplated suicide or murder to count fifty, and then go ahead and do it if he could. He reported twice a week and each time received the assurances that there were signs intelligible to the medical eye that he was better. He made a complete recovery in eight months.[40]

Unfortunately Center did not report the conversations that took place between himself and his patient; none of the case literature includes records of such discussions. It is clear that the physician's attitude of concern and optimism was considered more important than the text of the interview itself in building up the nervous patient's confidence. The outline of treatment described by Center, however, was but a variation on the theme that Mitchell had sounded with his rest cure treatment after the Civil War, and long known in medical practice. Physicians found combination treatments, including especially educational measures, effective in dealing with even severely distressed patients.

The nineteenth-century model of educational treatment was psychotherapeutical but not psychoanalytical; it differed in several respects from twentieth-century psychiatry. Although the subconscious mind was known to exist, there was little recognition of the unconscious. Dreams were troublesome only because they disturbed sleep and contributed to nervousness. Unpleasant thoughts were to be suppressed, and physicians believed firmly that patients not insane or completely degenerated through vice or heredity were capable of controlling their thoughts and emotions. While patients were encouraged to give a full accounting of their medical and family histories at their first visit, these were not explored in future conferences. Family relationships were seldom discussed, and patients were expected to overcome any temptation to dwell on their troubles.

The advice to "buck up" is anathema to much of psychological theory today, but nineteenth-century physicians routinely used this "common sense" method, apparently with some success. Analysts in the early twentieth century believed that the previous method of educational treatment had alienated patients and prevented physicians from identifying with their patients' suffering, but educational treatment did imply confidence in the patient's ability to achieve self-control. In this sense physicians minimized distinctions between the normal and abnormal; short of insanity, they believed, men and women were capable of directing their thoughts and overcoming their fears. The neurologist Theodore Diller, who wrote "Imperative Conceptions as a Symptom of Neurasthenia" in 1896, explained that "the term imperative conception is somewhat misleading in that the command it implies is by no means always obeyed. Morbid impulses may frequently and for many years arise in an individual and yet always be successfully resisted."[41]

Diller clearly believed that psychoses and neuroses were caused by intrusion of the subconscious into the conscious mind, and that mental health was determined by the individual's ability to resist and suppress irrational ideas:

> Probably in all of us impulses, fears, or doubts arise suddenly in consciousness as isolated thoughts or emotions, and which may be apparently totally disconnected with the mental state immediately preceding their appearance. For instance, many of us, I presume, have been seized with the desire to count the windows or doors in passing along a street, or in walking to avoid carefully the cracks in a pavement or to touch fenceposts. Looking from a great height the idea occurs to most persons to precipitate themselves below. The sight of a fragile piece of china or glassware suggests the idea that it could be readily crushed. A helpless child or a feeble invalid suggests how easily each could be killed. Certain words or phrases, lines of poetry or bars of music, may thrust themselves into consciousness at odd times.[42]

Diller distinguished abnormality as the inability to resist "action contrary to volition." Thus patients who refrained from committing acts that suggested themselves to the conscious mind were sane if not completely normal. Between the extremes of strong will power and none were "all gradations," Diller concluded, "and to say when an imperative conception ceases to be physiological or within the bounds of health would be as difficult as to say where sanity ends and insanity begins."[43]

Diller displayed a sophisticated understanding of psychological principles that were developing in the late nineteenth century and that were to become increasingly important in the next decades. His treatment programs—as demonstrated by the case below— likewise reflect a bridge between Beard and Freud. While he relied on several standard physical remedies, Diller also discussed the role of mental therapy, which he considered central to the outcome of the case:

A hard-working, robust-looking, professional man, aged twenty-nine years, was sent to me by Dr. W. F. Robeson last spring. Six weeks before, while sitting in the first balcony at the theatre, he experienced suddenly a strong impulse to pre- cipitate himself below. In great fear and agony he left the the- atre lest he should act upon the impulse. The next day he felt strongly impelled to break all the china upon the table. After this he was seized with many imperative conceptions, and his life was one of great distress to him, as he feared he was going insane. Examination revealed a long train of neurasthenic symptoms: headache, morning-tire, loss of endurance, irri- tability, insomnia, etc. He had worked very hard, frequently over-taxing himself, mentally and physically, since boyhood, and while he suffered from some of these neurasthenic symp- toms prior to the appearance of the sudden impulse and fear which came to him in the theatre, yet they were not marked, and he had almost wholly ignored them, and had in nowise drawn less on his nervous force in the prosecution of his work; but with the advent of these imperative conceptions his other neurasthenic symptoms became marked, and it was not difficult to discover them when I first saw him, and hence to recognize the morbid impulses and fears as belonging to them. . . .

Firm assurances as to the absence of organic diseases and harmlessness of these imperative conceptions, if the will- power were brought to bear, coupled with a semi-rest treat- ment, hydrotherapy, faradism, tonics, and occasional hypnot- ics, brought about in the course of six months a restoration of health. Several relapses, however, occurred, and for a time the patient was frequently seized with imperative conceptions of one sort or other; but with the assurances he had received they caused him much less fear.[44]

While modern standards of severity or chronicity cannot be applied to nineteenth-century case records, some records describe cases obviously of serious dimensions. Even these patients, physicians believed, could be treated successfully through reasoning and reassurance. In such instances it was the physician's will power that was exerted to gain control over the patient until he or she was strong enough to function independently. In a paper read at the Iowa State Medical Association meeting of 1886, Margaret Cleaves reported a case involving a patient who, in current psychiatric terms, would probably be diagnosed as suffering from pronounced anorexia nervosa. Cleaves's management of the case reflects the highest ideals of medical practice and the results that kind and determined treatment could produce. The patient was Miss ———, a girl of eighteen, with healthy parents but whose mother was of a neurotic temperament. As a child she was healthy, and at fifteen weighed 120 pounds, but after attending a girls' school where the pressure of lessons was heavy, Miss ——— began to feel constantly tired. Her appetite was poor; she was nervous, emotional, and often depressed. When she left school in April 1884 her menstrual periods had ceased, she had backache and headache, and threw up her food "once, twice, or three times a day." "Circulation poor, extremities cold, and her hands looked shrivelled and old. Nails were perfectly blue. Was restless during the day and sleepless at night. Was nervous, easily worried, and irritable; irregular in all her habits. . . ." When a physician and family friend who had known Miss ——— from childhood saw her around the end of the year, he "was so shocked by her appearance that he insisted upon something being done." This physician recommended Cleaves, who saw the patient at her home on January 27, 1885. Cleaves found Miss ——— to be pallid, with lips almost bloodless, pulse irregular, and extremities cold. Excessive vomiting, which had persisted for two years, had produced patches of abrasion on the mucous membrane of the mouth; though the girl was tall and "with a well made frame," she weighed only ninety-seven pounds.

The patient's mother believed her daughter's trouble stemmed from the reproductive organs, but Cleaves was convinced that the girl was suffering from "a profound nervous exhaustion," and that the local symptoms were the effect of the neurasthenia. In other words "she failed to menstruate simply because she had neither nervous energy to preside over that function nor vital fluid to lose." Cleaves felt that local treatment was not indicated, but rather rest, nutrition, fresh air, sunshine, tonics, and attention to all the habits of daily living. "Recognizing the hysterical element . . . although not so marked as in most persons who have similar experiences," Cleaves recalled, "I realized . . . that the vomiting was not only to be controlled by improving the nervous tone, [and] the condition of the stomach . . . but by the enforcement of superior will power." Therefore, when the patient asked what she should have for supper, Cleaves replied, " 'for one thing, beef steak broiled and underdone.' 'But I can't, I can't eat any warm meat, I shall throw it up.' I replied, 'Yes you can, and I expect the next time you see me you will be able to tell me that you ate and retained it'; and I further intimated that I should lose confidence in her if she should continue to throw up her food."

Cleaves went on to give "the most minute instructions" as to rest, sleep, diet, dress, and the activities which were to occupy the patient's time.

> I had her placed in a large, cheerful, airy room, with southern and eastern exposure, and directed that she should sleep alone. That every evening before retiring she should have a thorough rubbing and kneading of the muscles . . . and that just before the room was quiet for the night, she should have a glass of milk or a cup of beef tea, with a cracker as she tired of one or the other. Upon wakening she was to have a cup of Broma or Cocoa, and then to rest for half an hour. Then to have a sponge bath and brisk rubbing, after which rest in bed for nearly an hour. Then breakfast of some one of the many prepared grains as wheat germ, soft-boiled eggs, mutton chops,

or broiled beef steak, toast and butter, and a cup of coffee half cream. After breakfast rest in the sunshine. In the middle of the morning a glass of cold or hot milk, or a cup of beef-tea. Rest again.

Detailed instructions were given for the remainder of the day as well, and this regimen was repeated day after day with minor variations instituted as seemed appropriate. The diet included beef, mutton, fish and oysters, rice, baked potato, bread, butter, cream, crackers, eggs, milk, broma or cocoa, and a glass of wine with dinner. Other vegetables and meats, as well as fruits, pastries, and confections, were forbidden. The bowels were regulated with suppositories of ergot and belladonna, and the patient took "with benefit" a preparation of calisaya bark and phosphate compound. Cleaves prohibited all reading and writing, sewing and "fancy work," but permitted the patient to do some light housework. The air in her room was kept fresh and as much sunshine let in as possible. With this attentive care Miss ———— gained a pound per week and regained the color in her face and lips. She ceased complaining of the shooting pains and fatigue that had troubled her, and urination, which had been frequent and painful, became normal. She was relieved of headache and nervous irritability, slept better, and woke feeling refreshed. At the time of Cleaves's paper in 1886, she reported that her patient was "gaining rapidly . . . and promises to have her health fully re-established. In good time, I trust, nature will kindly take care of the special function [menstruation]. Meanwhile, her greatest good is to be obtained by such hygienic measures and medical remedies as are necessary to keep her in health, and conserve her nervous energies. Possibly menstruation may not return, but I think it will."[45]

Psychoanalysts in the early twentieth century charged that the methods employed by their predecessors accomplished only temporary good in neurotic patients, with new obsessions cropping up to replace the old. One of the benefits claimed for Freud's system was that it achieved permanent cures by allowing patients to gain insight into their own cases. It is impossible today, of course, to ascertain the truth of this criticism, but it is clear that nineteenth-century physicians believed their methods effective and frequently reported that patients remained well long after treatment. While psychoanalysis did offer a distinct alternative to nineteenth-century measures and often produced dramatic results where hypnotism and suggestion had failed, pre-Freudian physicians were not without successes themselves. Certainly the current perception of psychiatric methods before the turn of the century as crude, physically based, and unsympathetic is unfounded. At least in the treatment of the noninsane but mentally disturbed, physicians understood their patients' problems and treated them compassionately. As Cleaves remarked philosophically in 1886, "there is something terribly mysterious about human nature." Neurasthenia was a condition "often cruelly misunderstood," whose victims, numbering in the thousands, suffered as much as those with more tangible diseases. She believed that "no class of cases require such large charity, comprehensive insight and judicious management as these." To Cleaves, who knew the subject both as patient and physician, death was "a thousand times [better] than the pains, mental and physical, of neurasthenia."[46]

NOTES

1. Throughout this study ANA members will be referred to as neurologists. Neurologists who were not members of the ANA will be identified as independent neurologists. All other physicians will be identified by their specialty—when known—or simply as doctors, in which case the physician is presumed to be a general practitioner. Collectively this last group will be called the non-neurologists.

2. See Appendix B for a complete listing of patient occupations.

3. The decision as to which occupational group in which to place individual patients was made not simply on the nominal description but also on the way in which the reporting physician described the patient's responsibilities and social standing.

4. Cantharides, a toxic preparation of the crushed, dried bodies of the beetle Lytta vesicatoria (or Cantharsis vesicatoria) is perhaps better known as Spanish fly, which, when used internally in moderate doses, acts as a diuretic and stimulant to the reproductive organs, and is poisonous in large doses. Applied as a topical agent it burns the skin and is also referred to as "blister bug."

5. Joseph Collins and Carlin Phillips, "The Etiology and Treatment of Neurasthenia. An Analysis of Three Hundred and Thirty-Three Cases," *Medical Record*, 55 (1899), 414.

6. In one case sex could not be determined.

7. Of those whose marital status was reported, 110 were married and 52 were single. For the age groups most heavily represented in the neurasthenic literature—twenty-five through forty-five—marriage was and is the norm in the general population, and it is likely that most physicians would have considered single status more noteworthy than the married state.

8. Theodore W. Fisher, "Neurasthenia," *Boston Medical and Surgical Journal,* 86 (1872), 67.

9. George M. Beard, "Cases of Neurasthenia (Nervous Exhaustion), with Remarks on Treatment," *St. Louis Medical and Surgical Journal,* 36 (1879), 345–46.

10. Ibid., p. 347.

11. Barbara Sicherman, "The Uses of a Diagnosis: Doctors, Patients, and Neurasthenia," *Journal of the History of Medicine,* 32 (1977), 40.

12. William Goodell, "The Relation of Neurasthenia to Disease of the Womb," *Transactions of the American Gynecological Society,* 3 (1879), 34–35.

13. Ibid., p. 36.

14. L. Harrison Mettler, "Psychic State Accompanying Hystero-Neurasthenia," *Clinical Review,* 23 (1905–6), 249–50.

15. E. C. Kinney, "Nervousness," *Proceedings of the Connecticut State Medical Society,* 1885, p. 26.

16. Ibid., p. 25.

17. Arthur Conklin Brush, "Cerebral Neurasthenia," *Medico-Legislative Journal,* 15 (1897–98), 170–71.

18. Ibid., p. 177. For a discussion of the M'Naghten principle as applied in American law during the period, see Charles E. Rosenberg, *The Trial of the Assassin Guiteau: Psychiatry and Law in the Gilded Age* (Chicago: University of Chicago Press, 1968), pp. 54–74.

19. Charles W. Hitchcock, "Border Line Cases of Neurasthenia," *Journal of the Michigan State Medical Society,* 5 (1906), 586.

20. Hugh T. Patrick, "Neurasthenia," *International Clinics,* 8 (1898), 187–88.

21. Roberts Bartholow, "What Is Meant by Nervous Prostration?" *Boston Medical and Surgical Journal,* 110 (1884), 54–55.

22. Ibid., pp. 53–54.

23. A. D. Rockwell, "Neurasthenia and Lithaemia: Their Differential Diagnosis," *New York Medical Journal,* 47 (1888), 181.

24. Ibid., p. 182.

25. Francis B. Bishop, "Neurasthenia," *Transactions of the Medical Society of the District of Columbia,* 1897, pp. 375–76.

26. Patrick, "Neurasthenia," p. 187.

27. Francis B. Bishop, "Sexual Neurasthenia as It Stands in Relation to the Borderland of Insanity, and Insanity in General," *Virginia Medical Monthly,* 18 (1891–92), 757.

28. Frank D. Bain, "Nervous Prostration," *Transactions of the Ohio State Medical Society,* 1897, pp. 246–47.

29. Margaret A. Cleaves, "Neurasthenia and Its Relation to Diseases of Women," *Transactions of the Iowa State Medical Association,* 7 (1886), 166–67.

30. Ibid., pp. 165–66.

31. George M. Beard, "Traumatic Neurasthenia," *New England Medical Monthly,* 2 (1881–82), 248–49.

32. Edward Reynolds, "Gynecological Operations on Neurasthenics; Advantages, Disadvantages; Selection of Cases," *Boston Medical and Surgical Journal,* 162 (1910), 113.

33. Frederick Coggeshall, "The Relation of Local Disease to Nervous Disorders, Especially Neurasthenia," *New York Medical Journal,* 80 (1902), 532.

34. Ibid., pp. 534–35.

35. Joseph L. Bauer, "The Why and Wherefore of Nervous Prostration and Allied Habits: Some Typical Illustrations of the Exercise of Positive Individuality and Change of Habit," *St. Louis Medical Era,* 3 (1894), 2–4.

36. John P. C. Foster, "Suggestive and Hypnotic Treatment of Neurasthenia," *Yale Medical Journal,* 8 (1901–2), 20.

37. Ibid., p. 21.

38. Ibid.

39. Charles D. Center, "The Educational Treatment of Neurasthenics," *Illinois Medical Journal,* 7 (1904–5), 565.

40. Ibid., pp. 565–66.

41. Theodore Diller, "Imperative Conceptions as a Symptom of Neurasthenia," *Medical News,* 68 (1896), 38.

42. Ibid.

43. Ibid.

44. Ibid., p. 40.

45. Cleaves, "Neurasthenia," pp. 174–78.

46. Ibid., p. 179.

THREE

On the Verge of Bankruptcy

Articles on nervousness began appearing in medical journals after 1869, when George Beard published his first article on the subject in the *Boston Medical and Surgical Journal* and launched his campaign to gain a place for neurasthenia in contemporary practice. The trickle of articles published in the 1870s had become a flood by the mid-1880s and reached a peak between 1900 and 1910. The literature on nervousness appeared in a wide variety of medical journals. No publication had a monopoly on the subject, though a group of ten journals did publish almost a third (32 percent) of the articles on the disease. These journals, listed in order by frequency of publications on neurasthenia, were the *Journal of the American Medical Association, Medical Record, Boston Medical and Surgical Journal* (later *New England Journal of Medicine*), *Alienist and Neurologist,* the *Journal of Nervous and Mental Disease* (the American Neurological Association's official organ), *Medical News, New York Medical Journal, International Clinics, International Medical Magazine,* and *Illinois Medical Journal.* Over two-thirds of the literature appeared in other periodicals across the country, from local and state transactions to the proceedings of a variety of specialty societies. The widespread distribution of journal literature suggests that neurasthenia was a subject familiar to many physicians and that the community of physicians who treated the disease extended well beyond the 262 who published articles.

Almost one-third (ninety-seven) of the 332 articles published in medical journals between 1870 and 1910 had been presented originally as papers read at local medical society meetings. Many of these lectures were delivered by physicians who had been asked to research and report on the topic; they did not claim to be authorities on neurasthenia but relied heavily on textbooks in preparing their lectures. These pieces tend to be derivative but, because the authors frequently added observations from their own experience and sometimes took exception to authoritative views, they provide important clues to the acceptance of Beard's and other experts' theories among the general medical profession. Slightly over one-quarter (eighty-six) of the articles were papers originally read at state, regional, or specialty society meetings. The remaining 40 percent (130 articles) of the literature, except for a few pieces of correspondence, clinic reports, and assorted other addresses, consists of original articles submitted directly to medical journals. These articles represented new contributions to the literature on neurasthenia and frequently included case records from the writers' private or clinic practice.

The medical journal literature reveals a consensus among physicians about neurasthenia's symptoms and causes. Given the exhaustive catalogue of symptoms Beard attributed to the condition, it is striking that authors, whether ANA members, independent neurologists, or non-neurologists, reached agreement early on regarding the most important symptom categories, though most conceded that the list of possible symptoms was endless. Symptoms fell into two not-altogether-separable classifications, "physical" and "mental." Excessive fatigue from slight exertion was the primary sign of neurasthenia and characterized the illness, known also as nervous exhaustion and nervous prostration. Patients complained of fatigue so pronounced that they could arise only with extreme difficulty and could not attend to their usual affairs. Other physical symptoms cited were gastric disturbances and headache; a slightly less important group consisted of sensory disturbances, muscle and motor fatigue, weakness in the back and spine, temperature and circulatory problems, back pain, distress of the sexual apparatus, and dizziness and fainting spells. The most prominent mental symptoms were insomnia, lack of concentration, depression, fears, and irritability. Also mentioned frequently were restlessness, obsessions and illusions, and loss of self-control.

The difficulty of classifying symptoms as either physical or mental is obvious given the psychosomatic character of many complaints such as dyspepsia (indigestion) or fatigue, but physicians clearly made this distinction themselves despite the fact that most of the physical symptoms were subjective and hence not directly observable. Because the pathology of the disease remained an enigma, physicians sometimes paid inordinate attention to seemingly trivial complaints that might provide a clue. This was especially true of Beard and other early writers, but by the 1890s it was recognized that many of the physical symptoms of nervous patients were imaginary or psychosomatic, and that mental manifestations, particularly depression, were most crucial to diagnosis. The elusiveness of many complaints perhaps explains why physicians were also fond of reporting symptoms that were readily apparent, such as Beard's "neurasthenic voice," "changes of expression," coated tongue, and bad breath.

Beard had recognized neurasthenia primarily by the presence of physical complaints lacking a discoverable organic cause. This led him to weigh all symptoms equally and sometimes to attach undue importance to relatively minor problems. Later writers, less steeped in the somatic tradition in which Beard had been trained, dispensed with this abundance of detail. They not only categorized symptoms into several distinct groups, making diagnosis easier, but also recognized physical disorders as secondary to the emotional disturbance that characterized neurasthenia. The major symptom categories involved systemic functions and could be grouped as digestive, vascular, motor, sexual, mental, and sensory. Digestive symptoms included indigestion, variable appetite, coated tongue, constipation, or an irregular condition of the bowels. Vascular symptoms were manifested by irregular actions of the heart—palpitation, tachycardia (rapid heartbeat), and bradycardia (abnormally slow heartbeat)—hot flashes, coldness of the extremities and a mottled condition of the skin due to vasomotor disturbances, and polyuria, or excessive passage of urine. Among the motor symptoms were exaggerated knee-jerk, twitchings, and general nervousness; sexual signs included impotence, nocturnal emissions, spermatorrhea, and prostration after coitus. Sensory symptomatology included pains—especially headache and spinal tenderness—vertigo, and tingling sensations. By the 1890s mental symptomatology, and especially depression with its manifestations in insomnia, decreased sexual desire, lack of ability to concentrate, and obsessions and fears, had become the chief signs by which physicians recognized the American disease.

In a paper read before the Post-Graduate Clinical Society in 1890, the noted neurologist Charles L. Dana, then professor of diseases of the mind and nervous system in the New York Post-Graduate Medical School, presented a typical classification of neurasthenic symptoms. He listed first mental and sensory symptoms, then pains and neuralgias including headache and back pain, disturbances of the special senses, the motor and muscular system, and of the vasomotor, sexual, and digestive systems. In Dana's view the mental symptoms were most important and physical complaints almost entirely imaginary or psychosomatic, stemming from the underlying psychological element. Sexual problems, for instance, were caused by morbid fears that produced depression or inability. He held that neurasthenia was "a morbid condition of the nervous system whose underlying characteristics [were] excessive irritability and weakness," and noted that its victims suffered "from a peculiar feeling of nervousness, discomfort, uneasiness, and sense of unrest." The neurasthenic, said Dana, "loses interest in his work, dreads to undertake any responsibility, has morbid fears regarding his business, his sexual functions, his general health, his future, or some trivial subject. Some idea fixes itself upon him, and he cannot rid himself of it. He has difficulty in concentrating his mind on work. Periods of depression attack him. These mental states vary much, and may be so paroxysmal as to form 'crises.'"[1]

The increasing emphasis on depression as an important element in the diagnosis of neurasthenia was evident throughout all ranks of the medical profession. In 1893 the independent neurologist

John S. Leonhardt of Lincoln, Nebraska, argued that neurasthenia might begin as a local problem located in a single organ or faculty but that its tendency was to spread through the entire body. Although the manifestations of this condition were so numerous and varied that "the nouns and adjectives of our otherwise rich language are exhausted and new ones coined in order to more exactly and minutely describe the polymorphic ailment," the neurologist who knew what he was doing would look for the telltale signs by which the disease could be recognized. To diagnose the condition successfully the physician should keep in mind what Leonhardt called the neurasthenic coefficients—"sleeplessness, defective vision, sexual weakness, unnatural dryness of the skin and mucous membranes, excessive clammy perspiration of the hands and soles of the feet, morbid fears, and mental depression."[2]

In an 1899 article, Clarence W. Coulter, a general practitioner from Oil City, Pennsylvania, discussed the difficulty of treating neuroses in general and neurasthenia in particular. Coulter thought it next to impossible to classify neurasthenia's symptoms but noted the major symptom categories and particularly stressed the mental characteristics of the ailment. "The mentality of the neurasthenic is one of static depression. These patients lack power of mental concentration, are irritable, have a dread or fear of present or future happenings, which is undefinable; in fact," Coulter believed, "life to the neurasthenic is dotted with mythical absurdities and they are, in a word, pessimistic."[3] A Cleveland physician, Harry H. Drysdale, echoed these views in an article published in 1903. Drysdale observed that while some patients had sensory, motor, or secretory complications, the most notable feature of neurasthenia was "the marked despondency or lowspiritedness, often pitiable to observe and which often alternates with irritability and even anger." Some neurasthenics were suicidal, Drysdale said, and most were "hypochondriacal . . . imagining all forms of physical infirmities and many times . . . [fearing] insanity."[4]

Thus physicians of all types, in major cities and smaller communities across the country, were in agreement as to the symptomatology of neurasthenia. Although it might be difficult to diagnose because it could involve any or all of the body's functions, the key lay in the recognition of mental distress. While Beard had compiled a hodgepodge of undifferentiated symptoms to which he continually added new discoveries, it was neurologists like Charles Dana and James Jackson Putnam who recognized the significance of mental affections and particularly depression. Both Dana and Putnam described the psychological nature of neurasthenic symptoms and were leaders in the employment of "psychic" or mental treatment. By the turn of the century concepts of nervous disease were known and accepted by rank-and-file physicians; a diagnosis of neurasthenia implied both physical complaints without organic basis and, more important, mental symptoms such as depression, morbid fears (phobias), and "lack of vitality."

Most physicians agreed with Beard that they were witnessing the spread of a new disease, or at least one that had only recently become a problem in the rapidly increasing pace of American civilization. Though there was a growing recognition after the turn of the century that the malady was not uncommon on the Continent, many physicians continued to take pride in referring to neurasthenia as the "American disease" that proved the aggressive and competitive nature of American society. Neurasthenia was believed to be virtually unknown in the uncivilized world, and, oddly enough, most physicians agreed with the neurologists' assessment that the disease predominated among the brain-working class of the major cities, though many treated obvious exceptions to this stereotype at public dispensaries and in small-town offices throughout the country. The persistence of this view was probably caused by two factors: first, because the prestigious neurologists who most influenced professional opinion themselves saw wealthy patients in greater numbers, and, second, because class distinctions were often made by physicians between private and clinic patients. Ingrained class biases led many physicians to believe that the lower classes did not possess the high-strung nervous systems that produced neurasthenia, and dispensary cases, to whom relatively little time could be devoted, were doubtless frequently diagnosed as dyspeptic or hypochondriacal rather than nervous. While it was apparent (especially after 1900, when the disease's "popularity" surged) that poor patients, too, could suffer from neurasthenia, an explanation was offered to incorporate this inconsistency into existing theories of neurasthenia. Muscle-workers, it was argued, usually suffered from physical overwork which manifested itself in the spinal form of neurasthenia known as spinal congestion. The professional classes, who worked with their brains rather than their hands, were more likely to suffer from mental overstrain which produced cerebral neurasthenia.

The causes of neurasthenia, physicians agreed, were of two types—hereditary and acquired, with the influence of heredity being the most important predictor of the development of nervous disease. An individual's heredity acted as a predisposing cause, which could be triggered by acquired or precipitating factors including overwork, emotional stress like anxiety or grief, or even sudden shocks such as illness or fright. Heredity and acquired causes operated in inverse proportion to each other; the stronger the heredity the more pressure the individual could withstand before suffering a nervous attack, and vice versa. The belief in a finite inheritance of nervous energy was a concept important to the world view of nineteenth-century America as well as to the neurasthenic model. While popular thought in the Jacksonian period had emphasized the opportunities available to the common man, Americans of the late nineteenth century were beginning to realize the disappointing reality that there were limits to what each citizen could attain. They blamed these limitations on faulty inheritance; just as the insane could not be cured by "moral treatment," so neurasthenics could not be given more psychological strength ("nervous energy") to withstand the stresses of life. They had, instead, to be educated to live within their capacities.

American physicians in the late nineteenth century did not understand heredity solely in terms of genetic inheritance and did not have access, of course, to the concept of recombinant DNA, which revolutionized scientific thinking on the mechanism of biological inheritance in the twentieth century. Gregor Mendel's ideas had by the late 1800s made a significant impact on the scientific community in Europe, but the biological determinism central to Mendel's theories did not appeal to American physicians steeped in the Horatio Alger-like belief that individuals could rise above the station into which they were born. On the other hand, doctors could see as well as anyone else that children tended to resemble their parents, and it seemed only logical to assume that mental and emotional, as well as physical, traits could be transmitted from parent to child. Thus physicians, who, except for an elite few, were not well read in European scientific sources, gravitated naturally toward a brand of homespun Lamarckianism. They recognized inheritance of mental predispositions (believing that such tendencies could be caused as frequently by the prenatal environment as by biological factors), but they also believed that individuals could improve on their emotional inheritance and overcome all but the most odious inherited characteristics through will power and self-control, and could even pass on these acquired characteristics to their children. Class biases complicated this hereditarian optimism, however. Physicians, in common with other theorists on heredity, believed that the upper classes were higher on the evolutionary scale than the ignorant poor. The more cultured (and advanced) classes were capable of finer sensibilities, though they were likewise more susceptible to emotional stresses and strains than were members of the lower social orders. Like thoroughbred race horses, these nervously prepared individuals had to be protected from too much activity and from unnecessary emotional upsets.

Physicians frequently used metaphors of "nervous bankruptcy" to explain the limitations of psychological strength: such figurative language provided a visual image easily understood by patients and allowed physicians to indulge in literary flights of fancy; furthermore, it equated the disease with the spirit of American capitalism, which was thought to have contributed to its prevalence. In an address on neurasthenia in 1883, J. S. Greene, a Boston physician, provided his colleagues in the Massachusetts Medical Society with his own rendition of the idea that individuals who consistently "overdrew on their savings" risked nervous bankruptcy. "The patient may be likened to a bank," said Greene, "whose specie reserve has been dangerously reduced, and which must contract its business until its reserve is made good; or to a spendthrift, who has squandered his inheritance; or to a merchant, who has expanded his business beyond what his capital justifies, until he comes to the verge of bankruptcy. The one must collect promptly and shorten his credits, and otherwise gradually but steadily and resolutely restore his business to a safer basis; the other must rigidly limit his expenditure until it is sufficiently within his lessened income, with a margin for emergencies."[5]

The neurologist Charles H. Hughes, editor of *Alienist and Neurologist,* used much the same language in an address to the St. Louis Medical Society in 1894 when he described what he termed "this peculiarly American disease of the counting-house, the pulpit, the rostrum and the exchange." Neurasthenia, Hughes said, "is the disease which first overtakes the man of extensive business affairs and cares who egotistically regards his brain and connected nervous system as a perpetual motion machine not governed by the ordinary laws of supply and demand of nerve force, of waste and repair of energy." It was the disease, Hughes continued,

> of the man who not only expends the principal of his stored up nerve energy by drawing out all the reserve and exhausts the interest, [but] being unprepared for the unexpected bankruptcy finds himself involved in business affairs he no longer has the strength to satisfactorily conduct. The successful lawyer, the great jurist, the popular actor, the talented preacher, the successful politician, the skilled and publicly appreciated physician, the brilliant writer (sometimes he is an editor), the artist, the architect, the zealous tradesman, ambitious politician,—all and every one in every rank of life who runs for life's prizes without heeding the physiological warning on the wall, treat themselves in the same suicidal way as if there were for them no physiological reckoning, no pathological hereafter.[6]

Or as Dr. George R. Love of Toledo put it in 1905 in a paper read before the Academy of Medicine of Toledo and Lucas County: "So long as they are content to transact a moderate business with their life capital, all may go well. But there is no reserve, and [in] the emergencies which constantly arise in the pressing demands of our modern life these small capitalists go under and come to us as nervous bankrupts."[7]

Recognition of the laws of heredity was disappointing to Americans raised on the myth that any man could rise beyond his beginnings if he tried hard enough—a myth kept alive by the best-selling novels of writers like the prolific Horatio Alger. Nevertheless, the effect of inheritance on the individual's health was inescapably obvious to the observant physician. In a paper read before the Luzerne [Pennsylvania] Medical Society in 1903, Dr. B. G. Wetherby philosophized that "when we attended school we learned that 'all men are born free and equal.' This is not true, for men are born very unequal, and unequal they remain to the end of life." Wetherby recounted a recent eulogy delivered by an "eminent divine" on the life of William McKinley, at the close of which "a man well advanced in years . . . remarked that the good Bishop might have gone a little farther for the good of the young men present, and might have said that what McKinley did they, too, may do." But Wetherby thought the Bishop wise in stopping where he did. "Any man cannot be a McKinley or Lincoln, unless he is born with the right kind of stuff in him," he maintained; "such men are born, not made. McKinley and Lincoln were not neurasthenics."[8]

Thus some Americans would inevitably strive for more than they could reasonably attain. This was not necessarily a sign of weakness but an indication of aspirations for upward mobility and of finely tuned sensibilities. American nervousness was an affirmation of the American dream, the exception that proved the rule. The abundance of riches evident in every city and the promise of unlimited possibilities provided endless opportunities for acquired stresses to trigger neurasthenic attacks in the nervously ill-prepared. Physicians believed, however, that even in cases in which the hereditary taint was strong, much could often be done to relieve patients willing to be educated to "live within their means" of nervous energy, due to the direct relation between the inherited store of nerve capacity and the amount of life stress the individual could bear before breaking down.

The model of constitutional nerve capacity—the "nervous" or

"neuropathic diathesis"—was used to explain the fact that some individuals could withstand tremendous pressures while others collapsed under seemingly trivial strains. The concept was based on the idea that nerve strength could be inherited, stored, and passed on to offspring. Parents were held accountable for "husbanding" their own nervous energy so that their children would not be handicapped in the race of life, and children of nervous parents were especially warned to practice moderation to avoid breakdowns. Individuals who had once suffered a nervous attack also had to store up reserves of nerve force. This simplistic model was sensible but hardly scientific. While it sufficed as a metaphoric explanation of the processes that produced neurasthenia, physicians realized that a more precise understanding of pathology was necessary if they were to be able to cure or prevent the disease.

The first attempts to explain the physiological changes that took place in the neurasthenic's body were rather naive efforts to apply scientific terminology to purely theoretical discussions. The model of the neuropathic diathesis and concepts of nervous bankruptcy were incorporated into a "waste versus repair" theory that could be couched in impressive-sounding jargon, imbuing physicians with the aura of advanced scientific thinking. Like Beard's theories, these observations were based almost entirely on speculation, but this fact did not deter physicians from offering their views in the most technical manner possible.[9] Thus Dr. James Brown stated to the committee on pathology of the Wisconsin State Medical Society in 1878 that neurasthenia was caused by "a lesion of nutrition—not an anatomical lesion properly so called, but properly a defect in the molecular constitution of the protoplasm of the cells of the gray neurine, due to a molecular disintegration of this substance in excess of integration by the reparative process."[10]

The "waste versus repair" theory supplemented the nervous diathesis concept, but it was the work of physiologists studying live tissue in animals, beginning in the 1880s, that offered the first real promise that the pathology underlying nervous prostration would be discovered. A number of foreign physiologists, particularly Angelo Mosso of Italy, were frequently cited by physicians writing on neurasthenia, and the American Clifton F. Hodge of Clark University was recognized as the leading authority on the matter of nerve cell nutrition. Hodge, cited more often in the neurasthenic literature than anyone save Beard, demonstrated that pigeons and other animals dissected after exertion, and frogs subjected to the "artificial fatigue" of electrical stimulation, showed actual shrinkage in nerve cell tissue. This discovery was seized upon by neurologists as proving the organic basis of neurasthenia, and it seemed that the key to understanding the mysterious nature of nervous exhaustion was at hand. Their expectation was communicated to the medical profession at large, and physicians everywhere believed that research was in progress to explain the pathology of neurasthenia.

One of the most informed discussions of Hodge's work took place, surprisingly enough, at the Tri-State Dental Meeting of 1901, where dentists from Ohio, Michigan, and Indiana heard Will H. Whitslar read a paper on dental neurasthenia. After assessing the views of Ambrose Ranney, Francis Dercum, and Charles Dana on the nerve weakness and irritability that characterized neurasthenia, Whitslar explained the work of Mosso and Hodge. He reported Mosso's experiments demonstrating that fatigue altered the composition of the blood and that when a fatigued animal's blood was injected into an animal at rest the latter took on the characteristic symptoms of fatigue. Whitslar then turned to the work of Hodge, discussing specifically his 1892 article in the *Journal of Morphology* detailing experiments similar to Mosso's. "As an illustration," Whitslar reported, "the nerve cells of bees that had worked all day were compared with those of the same hive that had been resting during the same period. . . . In all instances, and in other animals upon which the same experiments were performed, changes were discovered in the nerve cells, and the changes were always the same. It was found that the nucleus of the cell decreases in size and becomes irregular in outline. The protoplasm of the cell shrinks, and spinal ganglia are vacuolated. The cell-capsule, when present, has a decrease in the size of its nuclei. Lastly, nerve cells recover if allowed to rest for a sufficient time, the recovery being slow." Whitslar concluded that "from the loss of cell substance there must be much waste product circulating in the blood, and, as related in the experiments of Mosso above quoted, the excessive material has a toxic action, and thus paralyzes the system. In other words, there is an auto-intoxication of the tissues from simple fatigue." [11]

The setting in which this technical discussion of physiological research took place—a regional dental convention—indicates how widely the work of Hodge and other physiologists was known. Hodge's research was attractive for several reasons: it was scientific, it complemented the preexisting model of inherited weakness combined with excessive strain, and it implicitly supported a major theme in American society—that moderation was the only sure path to health and happiness. These physiological discoveries, however, did not solve the mystery of nervousness as expected, and for one reason: there was, in fact, no research on neurasthenia taking place. Neurologists, like most modern practicing psychiatrists, did not conduct physiological research, and physiologists only touched on neurasthenia incidentally to other studies. Hodge's "body" of work on fatigue consisted of but two articles, which were not followed by further investigations. References to Hodge became more and more perfunctory in the 1900s, and his name was generally mentioned only briefly as proof that science was at work to solve the problem of neurasthenia. Neurologists and other physicians simply offered the evidence that scientific research was in progress and went on to the more urgent business of treating patients who suffered from the ailment.

Thus pathological research agreed that heredity acted as a predisposing factor that could fortify the individual against the stresses of modern life or alternatively render one susceptible to nervous attack. Many nineteenth-century physicians believed that the new urban way of life was producing generations of Americans with smaller reserves of nerve force and at the same time creating new and more intense strains, or precipitating causes, to threaten the individual from without. With all the demands of modern life—time schedules, rapid means of communication, the competition of the urban marketplace—it was little wonder that even normally strong individuals broke down. The precipitating or acquired factors that produced neurasthenia were cumulative and most often included overwork, anxiety, or grief. Sometimes these states existed for long periods until a seemingly unrelated incident such as illness, injury, or emotional shock triggered a neurasthenic attack.

New modes of transportation, for example, were frequently regarded as causes of so-called traumatic neurasthenia. Survivors of rail accidents and steamship disasters, though they may have survived the mishap without a scratch, might subsequently succumb to nervous prostration. While physicians observed that some victims made remarkable recoveries following favorable settlement of their lawsuits, they believed that the mental shock of accidents could leave long-lasting emotional scars. "Railway spine" was a common form of traumatic neurasthenia characterized by depression, lack of concentration, loss of memory, and weakness of the legs, back, and spinal cord. In one such case, reported by the eclectic Arthur H. Reading of Chicago in 1905, a young woman had fallen between the cars and the platform of a station while attempting to enter the elevated train. Her sister lifted her up by the shoulders into the car just as the train started, but the passengers "crowded around her and asked all manner of questions and made the young woman so nervous that she and her sister left the train at the next station, continuing their homeward trip on the next train."

The woman appeared well on the day following her accident, but a few days later Dr. Reading was summoned to find that the patient was "confined to her bed in a torpid state, and did not wish to be disturbed; complained of pain in the head, in her back, and in the shoulders. She had some nausea and vomiting; could not sleep well, did not care to eat; bowels inclined to be constipated; would not answer questions and had spells of crying, throwing about her arms and complaining of headache." These symptoms persisted for some days and gradually lessened, but the nervous crying spells still occurred whenever the patient was disturbed by a caller or a professional visit. She continued to lose weight and took little interest in her surroundings; two years after the accident,

Reading wrote, "we find this patient in about the same condition. In calling upon her I find that she sits in a bent or partly reclining position, twisting her fingers; looks pale and stupid . . ."; the young woman, who had been working in a necktie factory at the time of her accident, was now unable to sew or to read much, and could "play upon the piano now but very little." She was "able to help her mother wait upon customers in their little candy store some days" and had tried to ride on the streetcars three or four times, but "became so tired and was so nervous that it did not seem to do her any good. She shook all over, and fainted, the first time she went for a ride. . . . This patient," concluded Reading, "was a healthy young woman, and did not show any indication of nervous disease, but it is quite evident that now she is suffering with neurasthenia, caused by shock."[12]

Precipitating causes of neurasthenia such as trauma and grief were unavoidable or nearly so; at least individuals so afflicted were merely guilty of inheriting a nervous constitution that predisposed them to illness. Other causes involved habits of lifestyle and were either praiseworthy or damning according to the case and the physician's point of view. Because nearly all of the physicians writing on neurasthenia in the medical journals were partisans of the middle-class American ethic, their collective judgments on lifestyle causes of nervousness were of a pattern and amounted to a formidable body of professional opinion. Chief among the lifestyle factors causing nervous prostration was overwork, an excess physicians thought honorable and understandable, which they found most often in upper-middle-class business and professional men like themselves. In 1892 Dr. Edward Hornibrook of Cherokee, Iowa, reported on a typical case of overwork he had treated in 1879: "H. E., physician; age 40 years; has been in practice eighteen years; always worked hard; practice large; moderate and temperate in every respect." Hornibrook noted the patient never used alcohol "except to stimulate his flagging powers when over-fatigued. This occurs frequently, and the use of stimulants is always followed by headache. Had engaged one year previously in a political contest and a business enterprise with which he was unfamiliar." The patient also continued his practice, and soon found himself working an average of eighteen hours a day.

"During the first nine months of this unremitting labor," said Hornibrook, "he felt a sense of exhiliration [*sic*], self confidence and a capacity for work without fatigue. . . . It was no unusual thing to work at his profession for twelve hours, then address a public meeting, retire at 4 o'clock in the morning and commence work at 8. After a hard day's work at his profession, he would frequently spend the night in managing his business. Nine months of this unreasonable exertion was followed by headache and a sense of constriction around the head. He found that in adding up long columns of figures, his mind would become confused, his hand would sometimes tremble in the morning, there was a constant sense of weariness, he would find words misplaced in his business letters and syllables often dropped at the end of words. Cerebration became painful, bowels constipated, and digestion impaired." For these complaints Hornibrook advised rest and recreation, and abstention from tobacco "except in moderation." Under this treatment the patient gradually improved, "but for five years he had to avoid over-exertion or severe mental application." When Hornibrook reported the case in 1892, the patient was "in perfect health and . . . [continuing] to enjoy a large and lucrative practice."[13]

Hugh Patrick in 1898 reported the case of A. B——, an assistant professor "in an eastern college" who had consulted him some three years before and whose case demonstrated the relationship between heredity and environment. This single man, aged thirty-six, "was of even temperament, not impressionable, never an extremist, neither sanguine nor the reverse, of good habits and average mental capacity." The patient had educated himself and become first a country schoolteacher, then successively a teacher and principal of a town school. "Not satisfied with this he aimed to be a university professor—a laudable endeavor, it must be acknowledged, when coupled with adequate intellect. In the present instance it was ill-advised. Either the patient's natural capacity or his already existing brain-fag . . . [had] placed a lower limitation to his capabilities than that set by his ambition. In spite of this his aspirations and industry kept on overtaxing his brain until the point of marked insufficiency was reached. All his mental processes were sluggish, his 'reaction time' enormously increased, his work unsatisfactory to himself and others." Patrick felt that prolonged rest would have fully restored the patient, but as this was not practicable, "a compromise plan of materially diminished hours of work, materially increased hours of sleep, cold baths, and a reasonable amount of outdoor exercise" was worked out. Under this regimen the patient "greatly improved and has remained in good health. Of course," Patrick concluded, "the rational thing for him to do would be to return to the humdrum but less exacting life of the village teacher." [14]

The neurologist Sanger Brown, one of Patrick's Chicago colleagues, noted that "those influences which demand an exhaustive expenditure of nervous energy . . . are all the time rapidly increasing in professional, business and social life. The march of scientific progress is so rapid that the professional man has to maintain a high state of mental tension in order to keep pace with it, notwithstanding the mitigation afforded by specialism. Refinement in business methods, with the development of devices providing means of constant intercommunication, expose the business man to incessant drafts upon his capital of nervous energy; while keenness of competition, the added responsibility of success, as well as the anxiety and depression incident to failure, all contribute to neurenergenetic bankruptcy." [15] As Dr. William H. Williams of Lebanon, Indiana, put it, neurasthenia resulted from the "weight of anxiety, the mental strain of changing markets, and close hours of application to trade," all of which produced "strain [that] grows stronger and stronger until the once buoyant and cheerful body gives way to a swimming head, aching back, tired limbs, faulty digestion, sleepless nights and a shattered nervous system." [16]

Neurasthenia attributed to overwork occurred most often in men of the "better sort" whose natural ambition and competitive environment drove them to the breakneck pace and assumption of too many responsibilities that all too often led to nervous exhaustion. Some patients, however, were guilty of other excesses that led predictably, and more justly, to nervous disease. Chief among these causes were vicious habits—abuses of alcohol, drugs, tobacco, and the sexual function—and, in women, the attempting of work for which the weaker sex was unsuited. Overeating and lack of exercise, vices promoted by sedentary city life, also contributed to the sluggishness, constipation, and fatigue that characterized "lithemic" neurasthenia. These causes, wrote the neurologist Theodore Diller of Pittsburgh in 1902, could be categorized as "abuses of the mind and body—all departures from the normal, wholesome mode of living." [17]

Men who indulged in too-frequent sexual intercourse or who had practiced masturbation, even if only in adolescence, frequently believed that it was these habits that had caused their present unhappy state, and physicians did not disabuse them of this idea. Beard, who specialized in sexual neurasthenia in males, seldom inquired further into his patients' backgrounds once he had discovered evidence of masturbation. Though he usually did not derogate such patients, he clearly believed that "the evil habit" and sexual excess were frequent causes of neurasthenia. In 1891 Dr. Francis B. Bishop of Washington, D.C., upheld the common belief that masturbation sometimes led to insanity. "The patient," he said, "wanders, and lingers, perhaps for years, on the border of mental rapture and moral responsibility . . . [until he] eventually passes that imaginary line, . . . through a portal which has for its motto that which is said to have greeted the eyes of Dante, as he passed the entrance to the infernal region, 'Abandon hope, all ye who enter here. . . .'" [18]

In light of such dire predictions of doom, it is little wonder that masturbators feared insanity as the just deserts of their sin. Dr. Malcue G. Thompson, in an address to the Arkansas Medical Society in 1904, explained the guilt that commonly afflicted habitual masturbators. "Sexuality plays a great part in the development of neurasthenia, for in every brain is planted a sexual entity, and without the mind being properly employed we have an over-development of this entity rushing [young men] into excess or perversion, often at an age that the nervous system cannot stand the strain.

Not only have we this to contend with, but [also] the advertisement of the advertising doctor, exaggerating the sin and danger of this condition. They are educated to believe that punishment is a just retribution, and I have seen them that had read these advertisements until they not only had sexual neurasthenia but a sexual mania."[19]

Dispensary patients, among whom young males were disproportionately represented, were especially likely to be diagnosed as sexual neurasthenics if mental distress were evident. In 1903 the pharmacologist John V. Shoemaker remarked on the frequency with which young men were seen at his Philadelphia clinic suffering from neurasthenia "dependent upon irritation of the sexual apparatus consequent upon solitary vice or excessive venery."[20] The neurologist Bernard Sachs demonstrated a typical case of sexual neurasthenia in the New York Polyclinic in 1891. The patient, a car cleaner, was twenty years of age and a Russian by birth. He suffered from seminal emissions at night and on urination, "rushes of blood to different parts of the body," pains in the stomach, pains in the right side, and pains in the back; in fact, said Sachs, there was "scarcely an organ in his body" that did not exhibit some sort of symptom. The man admitted to frequent sexual intercourse, having begun his sexual career at sixteen and "worshipped freely at the shrine of Venus" since then. He claimed that he had never masturbated, but, remarked Sachs, "we can safely doubt that statement." "Similar histories we have to listen to frequently enough," Sachs went on, "especially in private practice. His symptoms are tired feeling in the morning, pains in the back and head, peculiar sensations in the arms and legs, a hot feeling in the testicles, a peculiar feeling in the stomach and in his eyes."

Sachs thought two symptoms especially indicative of neurasthenia—pressure on the top of the head and "peculiar feelings" in the nape of the neck, but he also noted mental depression and peculiar feelings in the spine. He pointed out a slight tremor in both "orbiculares" when the patient was asked to close his eyes, and tremors of the facial muscles. Sachs held that the same condition often presented whether the neurasthenia was caused by overwork, mental fatigue, or vicious habits; in the present case it was the history of sexual excess that indicated the diagnosis of sexual neurasthenia. To distinguish between the various forms of neurasthenia the physician had "in the majority of cases . . . to depend upon the history of the patient . . . ," making it likely that doctors would rely on stereotypes in diagnosing different forms of nervousness. Thus it was easy for Sachs to conclude that "neurasthenia from fatigue affects men who do too much work—physicians who are driven day and night, and merchants who are overworked during the day and have to travel in sleeping-cars at night," while young men whom he encountered in his clinic and office practice might be branded as perverts for the same symptoms.[21]

While in men precipitating causes such as mental overwork and vicious habits predominated, the causes of neurasthenia in women were most often biological and resulted from the upsetting of their more delicate nervous equilibrium. Beard had distinguished two forms of neurasthenia—cerebral and spinal—that, in his view, occurred frequently along gender-distinct lines. Men were likely to acquire the mental symptoms of "cerebrasthenia" that resulted from overuse of the brain and/or perversion. Although they could also acquire the spinal form, "myelasthenia," through physical exhaustion or trauma, this form of neurasthenia more commonly afflicted women; women's reproductive apparatus and menstrual cycles predisposed them to the spinal weakness and back pain that characterized spinal congestion. Physicians also believed that women's intellects were less well developed than men's and that the female brain was subservient to the more complex reproductive system.

Though Beard considered male patients his most difficult cases, he believed there were more female neurasthenics; this conviction was shared by gynecologists. Other physicians—particularly genitourinary specialists—held that the disease predominated in men, while still others claimed that both sexes suffered equally. Of the patients reported in medical journals between 1870 and 1910, males and females are recorded about equally (with men being reported only slightly more frequently), but it is clear that physicians perceived differences in both the symptoms and causes of neurasthenia in women. In his 1890 address to the Post-Graduate Clinical Society, Charles Dana argued that "neurasthenia is a severer disorder in women than in men, for the reason that the nervous system of woman is naturally less stable and less under volitional control. . . ."[22]

In a clinical lecture delivered at the Cincinnati Hospital in 1899, the noted gynecologist Charles A. L. Reed described the interdependent relationship that existed between the female genital and nervous systems: "[The] great sympathetic [nerve] . . . furnishes an abundant supply of branches directly to the womb, the ovaries, the vagina and the external genitalia." The significance of this was that "the genital organs of women, considered in the aggregate, are nothing more or less than a central telegraphic office, from which wires radiate to every nook and corner of the system, and over which are transmitted messages, morbific or otherwise, as the case may be; and it should be remembered right here that telegraphic messages travel both ways over the same wire; that there are both receiving and sending offices at each end of the line."[23] Woman's lack of nervous control, it was held, proved that her personality was directly linked to her uterus, an idea with wide currency during this "age of the womb."[24]

Physicians typically held ideas consistent with middle-class morality regarding woman's proper place. Elements of the medical profession, representing the spectrum from urban specialists to country practitioners, used the image of nervous invalidism to speak out against the emergence of the "new woman." Women were particularly likely to succumb to neurasthenia, it was thought, if they left the sphere of home and family. This was especially true of women who attended college or took part in too many social functions. Even the pressures of running a busy household could result in nervous prostration; women's constitutional delicacy predisposed them to nervousness. As the gynecologists Henry B. Deale and S. S. Adams stated in a paper read before the Washington [D.C.] Obstetrical and Gynecological Society in 1894, "[neurasthenia can strike] a young girl or woman harassed by the ambitions of school life or social excitements, or annoyed with household and family cares . . . , all occurring early in a time of life when the entire organism, nervous as well as physical, is undergoing a great strain—all this seems sufficient to account for the nervous depression or exhaustion that so frequently results."[25]

Sanger Brown, writing in 1901, agreed that social and family obligations threatened the health of American women.

> [If] the increasing complexities of modern civilization offer a menace to the neurons of business and professional men which may fairly excite concern, what shall be said of their effect upon the neurons of the modern society woman, with her perpetual breakfasts, luncheons, receptions and card parties; her clubs with their educational, municipal and philanthropic departments? And even under the weight of these great burdens, yielding to primitive impulses, she may attempt to divert some energy to the family circle, as, for instance, personal supervision of the housekeeping, the training and education of her children, etc. In her efforts to meet all these demands besides the many others which I have not enumerated, her liability to neurasthenia is positively alarming, and accordingly, sooner or later, she is likely to register at a rest cure.[26]

Brown doubtless hoped to attract some of these victims to his own establishment, Kenilworth Sanitarium, located just north of Chicago.

In an 1898 address to the Mississippi Valley Medical Association, Dr. Harry C. Sharp of Jeffersonville, Indiana, blamed neurasthenia in women on the domestic surroundings and social life of the patient. Sharp believed that the average woman "feels her life depends upon her social success. . . . [She] also feels that her position is very uncertain, . . . that unless she is ever pleasant and pleasing to the eye, she may be entirely forgotten, . . . a thing in her judgment justifiable of great grief, sorrow and much worry. With this [idea] firmly fixed in her mind, she enters upon her life work with the devotion of the business man, the feelings of uncertainty of the politician and the forgetfulness and disregard of self of the student, which is made up of one continuous round of excitement, pleasure, disappointment, and dissipation."[27]

Neurasthenia was "a positive argument against higher education of women," wrote Dr. S. W. Hammond of Rutland, Vermont, in 1908.[28]

Just as changes in women's roles threatened the stability of the family, according to many physicians, so too did changes in education. City school systems were failing in their mission to develop healthy and well-balanced citizens and thus posed a threat to the future mental health of the country. Unlike the small country schoolhouses that many physicians had known as children, city public schools were overcrowded and poorly ventilated; moreover, they ignored individuality and forced children too early into the competitive mainstream. I. P. Willits, an independent neurologist who served at Philadelphia's Germantown Hospital, mourned the loss of the idyllic rural childhood in a speech to the Medical Society of Germantown in 1897. Willits feared the new methods of schooling disregarded the well-known principle that the "nervous equilibrium is much more easily disturbed in children . . . than in adults" and would produce generations of unhealthy, nervous Americans.

"Cramming" and examinations caused worry and mental strain, said Willits, and he went on to catalogue the bad effects that modern schools had on the child's vulnerable nervous system: "eyestrain from ocular defects and bad light, bad habits of posture, bad ventilation, . . . overcrowding, the driving methods of teaching, the efforts of emulation and ambition, a totally bad system of education arising from the fact, probably unavoidable, that individual instruction is lost in class-instruction, and that all sorts of minds and abilities are forced to adapt themselves to a single standard." It was unfortunate that "we [physicians] cannot revolutionize the school system . . . ," he continued, for "little or no chance is given the teacher to understand her pupil as an individual, and it would be merely by an accident that the latter would be led through proper and healthy mental channels. 'Mere accident' will, of course, fail to find nine-tenths of the scholars, and these nine-tenths are compelled to obtain their education—the very word becomes a misnomer—by inapplicable methods, which, kept up for years throughout the whole length of school-life, foment a mental discord. . . ."[29]

Dr. E. C. Kinney, in his 1885 presidential address to the Connecticut State Medical Society, compared the school system to a factory, a common metaphor in the latter nineteenth century. Kinney criticized the new graded schools for overlooking the profound differences between pupils and creating a dull and unhygienic environment. He feared that overpressure in city schools posed a threat to the race's future; the schools, in the words of a teacher cited in his talk, were "educating a race of invalid mothers." Kinney advocated more physical exercise in urban, graded schools and noted that the ruddy complexions and robust physiques of children trained in one-room schoolhouses presented a sharp contrast to the pale and sickly products of city institutions. The country youth, he maintained, was "superior to the city boy for business or for a liberal education, not because he knows more, for he really knows less about many things, but because he is better developed . . . [and] approaches more nearly to the standard of perfect manhood, 'a sound mind in a sound body.'"[30]

Clearly the "American disease" was attributed to a multiplicity of causes that were inextricably associated with American society in the late nineteenth and early twentieth centuries. Sexuality, middle-class morality, and traditional values of moderation all contributed to perceptions of neurasthenia and its causes. But the overriding concerns of the physicians who treated neurasthenia were, first, the inability of individuals to escape their mental inheritance and, second, the fear of change and its ultimate consequences for the nineteenth-century way of life. The competition of the marketplace and the university, the mass production of the factory and the public school, the beckoning call of the city with its opportunities for vice as well as profit—all conspired against emotional

health. Physicians sounded a warning that has been a theme of tra-
ditionalists throughout history, namely, that the old ways are best
and that change, if unavoidable, should at least be gradual.

The emphasis on moderation and the belief that cities with their
concentration of vices posed a threat to mental health were common themes in nineteenth-century literature. To physicians, the
consequence of excess was, if not death or insanity, at least nervous
exhaustion. Because neurasthenia, once acquired, could seldom be
completely cured, physicians assumed the role of teachers or even
missionaries to educate their fellow Americans on the prevention
of neurasthenia. For the general public, who had not yet succumbed
to nervous prostration, this outreach work was accomplished
through public lectures and the medical advice literature so prevalent in the period. Dr. Willis F. Hart of Camden, Maine, for example, wrote in 1895 that physicians should take an active role in
teaching proper habits to minimize the influence of inherited tendencies, especially in the young. Physicians, he held, should teach
"that the laws of health cannot be violated without [*sic*] impunity,
but that they or their children will receive the penalty. Teach them
how to train the boys and girls so that when maturity is reached
they are fitted, body and mind, for active duties of life. Teach that
labor is honorable for all, idleness a disgrace. That the noblest
work of God is man as God intended him to be, well developed
physically, mental faculties clear and strong, and in all respects
able to perform life's duties, whether they be those of an ordinary
laborer or a philosopher. Teach all that to retain health and ability
to accomplish the most, regular periods of rest are necessary.
When all this is done," he claimed, "we shall find humanity better
able to endure hardships and adversities."[31]

Physicians agreed that heredity was the predisposing cause of
neurasthenia and that the stronger the history of hereditary nervousness the more careful the individual must be of excess, stress,
and shock. But as the independent neurologist Johann Flintermann
said in a paper delivered to the Detroit Medical and Library Association in 1898, moderate habits could minimize the influence of
heredity: "the hereditary taint does not always and absolutely lead

to the development of pronounced neurasthenia." Flintermann alleged that "there are cases of decidedly inherited disposition wherein, in consequence of a well conducted life and other happy circumstances, not a single symptom of nervous affection becomes noticeable."[32]

Individuals who were already victims of neurasthenia, however, needed considerable personal attention from their physicians, and often for an extended period of time. For them, advice literature was not enough; they could not possibly regain their health through self-help manuals alone. If anything, they required more care than patients whose illnesses were entirely physical; their care involved both treatment of immediate symptoms and education to minimize the risk of future attacks. In this respect, there was a distinguishable difference between physicians and popular writers on neurasthenia who emphasized self-help. Physicians clearly did not believe in self-help for those once stricken with nervous exhaustion and felt that such patients must be carefully nursed back to health and educated to live within their means of nerve force. The painstaking education of neurasthenics might take months or even years, and physicians feared lest distraught patients turn to irregular healers like Christian Scientists who, they were sure, would exploit their suffering.

Neurasthenics, like alcoholics, had to be led back to health and taught to guard against future attacks. Physicians sometimes went to great lengths to protect their neurasthenic patients from the rigors of modern life. An extreme example of the solicitude shown neurasthenics is provided by an article written by Charles Hughes that appeared in *Alienist and Neurologist* in 1904. Hughes wrote to inform other physicians of the attractions of the Louisiana Purchase Exposition which had recently opened in St. Louis ("this blended and unequaled picture of landscape and architectural beauty and commercial and educational utility, such as the world has never seen before in one assemblage and whose like perhaps we shall never see again") and also to warn them of the dangers that such an event might pose to their neurasthenic patients. "If . . . we consider . . . the magnificent distances and multiform attractions . . . and the expenditure of neuropsychic and muscular force necessary to see and hear [the exhibits] completely," Hughes cautioned, "we should say . . . the neurasthenic should not go there."[33]

If neurasthenic patients were intent upon making the visit, however, Hughes advised physicians on how the trip could best be managed. The patient should approach at the southeast gate, which afforded a view of the ground below; if necessary he should spend a full day enjoying the scenery and conserving energy before attempting the entrance. Once inside, he should visit no more than one building a day, "and then not without a roller chair," after which he might take a restful ride on the lagoon launches or gondolas, have luncheon, and retire to a suburban hotel for the remainder of the day. Viewing the entire exhibition on this plan would take from forty to sixty days, but Hughes believed that such caution was necessary. "To the neurasthenic," Hughes concluded, "a visit to this greatest of World's Universal Expositions is a risky experience, unless taken under neurologic advice and with due experienced psychiatric precautions."[34]

This advice repeats the theme that the nation itself—its new technologies, new patterns of working and living, and new perils as well as possibilities—could be a threat to mental health. As Dr. William O. Stillman remarked to the Albany Academy of Medicine in 1879, neurasthenia was the inevitable result of American civilization. "In America," Stillman averred, "industry is stimulated by vast opportunities," [and] "with illustrious examples of intellectual and commercial success before his eyes, the average American cannot resist thinking he may attain to the same likewise. It is constant push, and drive, and energy, until the poor machine gives out." Who "shall say that our boasted opportunities and broad avenues of success are not a curse instead of a blessing, if they bring this terrible visitant to our door—are not as fatal to our health and happiness as the fabled gift of Midas."[35]

Although physicians frequently claimed that the disease was misunderstood by a large segment of the profession, most doctors believed that they could diagnose and treat neurasthenia correctly. Published accounts of the discussions that frequently followed presentations at local and regional meetings clearly indicate that neurasthenia had an accepted place in medical nomenclature. Local physicians of all types were familiar with the literature and relevant research on the disease and took turns recounting their own experiences with patients. Few argued that so-called neurasthenics were malingerers, hypochondriacs, or anything other than what Beard had called them.

The medical journal literature on neurasthenia makes clear that physicians in all geographical areas and of a wide variety of specialties understood nervous disorders in similar terms. Their attempts to classify numerous symptoms as a single disease sometimes led to strained distinctions, but their recognition of psychological symptoms and causes of nervousness was an important element of psychiatric knowledge. Moreoever, this knowledge was as available to country doctors and general practitioners as to urban neurologists; there were no significant differences between ANA members, independent neurologists, and non-neurologists in their perceptions of neurasthenia.

Most physicians were firmly grounded in the middle-class ethos that formed the basis of their own backgrounds and experiences. This orientation affected their perceptions of neurasthenia; the lack of pathology left gaps in scientific knowledge that doctors filled with empirical observations, biases, and sometimes sheer imagination. Still, the solid social values held by most physicians provided a frame of reference that was useful to many nervous patients. Such patients benefited from the guidance of therapists who had confidence in the system and were secure in their own roles as healers and citizens. As the next chapters demonstrate, this self-assurance was an important element in the treatment of neurasthenia and in the subsequent development of modern American psychiatry.

NOTES

1. Charles L. Dana, "Neurasthenia," *Post-Graduate*, 6 (1890–91), 26.
2. John S. Leonhardt, "Neurasthenia; Remarks on Its Symptomatology," *Nashville Journal of Medicine and Surgery*, 74 (1893), 104–5.

3. Clarence W. Coulter, "Neurasthenia from the Standpoint of a General Practitioner," *Buffalo Medical Journal*, 39 (1899–1900), 84.

4. Harry H. Drysdale, "Neurasthenia, Its Etiology, Symptomatology and Treatment," *Medical Critic*, 2 (1903), 515.

5. J. S. Greene, "Neurasthenia: Its Causes and Home Treatment," *Boston Medical and Surgical Journal*, 109 (1883), 77.

6. Charles H. Hughes, "Neurotrophia, Neurasthenia and Neuriatria," *Alienist and Neurologist*, 15 (1894), 215.

7. George R. Love, "The Mental Factor in Neurasthenia," *Toledo Medical and Surgical Reporter*, 31 (1905), 423.

8. B. G. Wetherby, "Neurasthenia," *Transactions of the Luzerne County Medical Society*, 11 (1903), 10.

9. Beard often cited the work of DuBois-Reymond, published in the 1850s, regarding the dephosphorization that took place in the body during excessive toil, as part of his attempt to explain the nature of nervous exhaustion. John S. Haller and Robin M. Haller, *The Physician and Sexuality in Victorian America* (Urbana: University of Illinois Press, 1974), p. 10.

10. James Brown, "Neurasthenia, or Nervous Exhaustion," *Transactions of the Wisconsin State Medical Association*, 12 (1878), 107.

11. Will H. Whitslar, "Dental Neurasthenia," *Dental Cosmos*, 43 (1901), 1181.

12. Arthur H. Reading, "Shock: Causing Neurasthenia," *Chicago Medical Record*, 38 (1905), 516–18.

13. Edward Hornibrook, "Neurasthenia," *Transactions of the Iowa State Medical Society*, 9 (1892), 118–20.

14. Hugh T. Patrick, "Remarks on the Treatment of Neurasthenia," *Medicine*, 5 (1898), 198.

15. Sanger Brown, "Etiology of Neurasthenia," *Chicago Medical Recorder*, 20 (1901), 314.

16. William H. Williams, "Neurasthenia," *Medical and Surgical Monitor*, 6 (1903), 108.

17. Theodore Diller, "Some Observations on Neurasthenia," *Pennsylvania Medical Journal*, 5 (1902), 642.

18. Francis B. Bishop, "Sexual Neurasthenia as It Stands in Relation to the Borderlands of Insanity, and Insanity in General," *Virginia Medical Monthly*, 18 (1891–92), 754.

19. Malcue G. Thompson, "Neurasthenia," *Transactions of the Arkansas Medical Society*, 28 (1904), 131.

20. John V. Shoemaker, "Neurasthenia," *Medical Bulletin*, 25 (1903), 389.

21. Bernard Sachs, "Functional Nervous Troubles: Neurasthenia, Its

Occurrence in Young and Old, Symptomatology and Treatment," *International Clinics,* 1 (1891), 237–38.

22. Dana, "Neurasthenia," p. 32.

23. Charles A. L. Reed, "The Genital Factor in Certain Cases of Neurasthenia in Women," *Gaillard's Medical Journal,* 70 (1899), 68.

24. This phrase is borrowed from Sarah Stage, who borrowed it from Jules Michelet's *L'Amour.* See Stage, *Female Complaints: Lydia Pinkham and the Business of Women's Medicine* (New York: W. W. Norton & Co., 1979), pp. 64–88, for a discussion of medical attitudes toward women during the period.

25. Henry B. Deale and S. S. Adams, "Neurasthenia in Young Women," *American Journal of Obstetrics,* 29 (1894), 191.

26. Sanger Brown, "Etiology of Neurasthenia," p. 314.

27. Harry C. Sharp, "Neurasthenia and Its Treatment," *Journal of the American Medical Association,* 32 (1899), 72.

28. S. W. Hammond, "Neurasthenia," *Vermont Medical Monthly,* 14 (1908), 158.

29. I. P. Willits, "Some Causes of Nervous Phenomena in Children," *Philadelphia Medical Journal,* 2 (1898), 294.

30. E. C. Kinney, "Nervousness," *Proceedings of the Connecticut State Medical Society,* 1885, p. 41.

31. Willis F. Hart, "Neurasthenia," *Transactions of the Maine Medical Association,* 1895, pp. 160–61.

32. Johann Flintermann, "Neurasthenia," *Physician and Surgeon,* 20 (1898), 408–9.

33. Charles H. Hughes, "The Louisiana Purchase Exposition, The Neurasthenic and the Brain-Tired," *Alienist and Neurologist,* 25 (1904), 491.

34. Ibid., p. 497.

35. William O. Stillman, "Neurasthenia," *Medical and Surgical Reporter,* 40 (1879), 398.

FOUR

Not the Physic but the Physician

While the symptoms and causes of neurasthenia were relatively clear to most physicians, medical consensus ended when it came to treatments. Because all agreed that the treatment must be tailored to the needs of the individual patient, physicians experimented widely in prescribing therapeutic regimens, employing variations of those touted by colleagues and adding personal touches of their own. Much of the journal literature reports therapeutic methodologies which the authors had found particularly effective in treating various forms of the disease. Most treatments were aimed at relieving the specific symptoms that most often characterized neurasthenia—insomnia, constipation, fatigue, indigestion—and fell into several major categories. These treatments included rest, regulation of the diet, exercise either active or—in a form such as hydrotherapy—"passive," and drugs to aid digestion, enervate the nervous system, or induce sleep as the case required.

Beard offered few details of his own therapeutic techniques, outside of his instructions for applying the electric current that was his trademark and his early endorsement of psychological treatments such as suggestion. He was far more interested in understanding the nature of neurasthenia through its symptomatology and its causes than in attaching his name to particular therapies. Beard often stated that neurasthenia was relatively easy to manage, if not to cure, once it was properly diagnosed, and so directed his attention to discovering all the symptomatology by which it might be recognized. His case records reflect his impatience with the subject of treatment, and frequently contain but a line or two summarizing his methodology and results. In one record, for example, he reported merely that "I treated this case similar [*sic*] to other cases of that kind that I had cured, by the *interrupted* galvanic current in the inner angle of the eye with the negative pole, the positive being placed at the back of the neck, or on the temples. Immediate relief followed a single application, as it often will in a case of this kind, and I repeated the applications; but there was not that permanence in the effect that I desired." [1]

As the literature on neurasthenia grew, however, so too did the specificity of therapeutic methodologies. The basic types of treatment remained constant throughout the period from 1870 to 1910, although some therapies declined in relative popularity while others increased markedly. The ten most commonly applied treatments for neurasthenia, as determined by frequency of endorsement by physicians, were: rest, drugs, "mental" therapies, dietary regulation, hydrotherapy, electrotherapy, massage, exercise, travel, and general hygiene management. The increasing emphasis on mental therapeutics as understanding of the disease progressed in the latter part of the century is illustrated by the greater reliance on treatments like rest and travel by the 1900s. The table below demonstrates the relative decline of physical treatment from the 1870s to the 1900s:

Table 3. Recommended Treatments

1870s	1900s
1. Drugs	1. Rest
2. Rest	2. Travel
3. Electrotherapy	3. Mental (psychological)
4. Diet	4. Drugs
5. Exercise	5. Diet
6. Massage	6. Exercise
7. Mental (psychological)	7. Hydrotherapy
8. Hydrotherapy	8. Electrotherapy
9. General hygiene	9. Massage
10. Travel	10. General Hygiene

These therapies were not mutually exclusive, and their classification often represents the major emphasis of treatment rather than distinct categories. Most physicians employed several remedies; it was a successful combination of treatments that was sought and communicated to colleagues through the journal literature. Most physicians thought single-cure theories simplistic and argued that these defeated the purpose of treatment, which was to reeducate the patient to health. The physician's role, they believed, lay in prescribing a carefully planned daily regimen for each patient, which had the dual effect of reordering the lifestyle along more healthful lines and demonstrating that the physician had the problem well in hand.

Such was the essence of the Weir Mitchell rest cure, the only therapeutic formula to be applied systematically and to gain widespread acceptance during the period. Mitchell had developed his treatment during the Civil War for soldiers suffering from battle fatigue, but in the 1870s he extended its application to severe cases of neurasthenia and hysteria. Mitchell's cure consisted of complete bed rest, tonics, passive exercise in the form of massage or electrotherapy, and a strict diet high in protein and based on milk products to build up the weight and nerve force. The most important element of treatment, however, was the total isolation of the patient from all but the doctor and a trained nurse. This technique ensured that instructions would be followed to the letter and that the patient would be psychologically dependent on the physician. Mail was frequently excluded from the sick room, as was "any communication . . . except through the mouth of the doctor. . . ."[2]

The patient undergoing the rest cure should ideally be removed from the home environment, according to Mitchell. He and other neurologists operated private sanitariums at which the requisite strict discipline could be imposed. These clinics came to be regarded as resorts to which the fashionable, almost always women, could retire to "get away from it all." Such retreats provided their owners with substantial supplements to the fees they received from house calls and office practice. The patient was ordered to bed, from which she was forbidden to rise for any reason, including purposes of elimination, and was initially not permitted even to feed herself or to turn in bed without the assistance of the nurse. Massage and other forms of passive exercise were employed to prevent atrophy of the muscles subjected to total inactivity. Regarding his treatment, Mitchell said, "I do not hesitate to assert, as the result of a vast number of cases, that it is a resource of immense value. . . . We know most thoroughly that in the hands of firm, tactful, self-reliant physicians it will be rewarded with a large percentage of success."[3]

Mitchell based his rest cure on the scarcely disguised supposition that neurasthenia in women was self-induced and could be overcome if the patient really tried. As Barbara Sicherman has pointed out, it is not surprising that Mitchell's most notable therapeutic failures were women like Charlotte Perkins Gilman and Jane Addams, who rejected both the paternalism inherent in the rest cure and the subordinate role assigned their sex.[4] Gilman and Addams were less likely than most to succumb to what Sarah Stage has called the reverse psychology of Mitchell's cure, with its reliance on enforced boredom to return women to their "proper place."[5]

Gilman was induced by her husband to take the rest cure when she became intensely depressed following the birth of her daughter. Mitchell advised her to give up her writing career and devote herself exclusively to motherhood and domestic responsibilities. However, the cure backfired when Gilman rebelled against the psychological torture of enforced isolation. She divorced her husband and wrote a short story, "The Yellow Wallpaper," describing her experiences with Mitchell's treatment. In the story the heroine is driven insane by her confinement in a room with yellow wallpaper.[6]

The psychological nature of the rest cure was especially apparent in the regulation of the diet. The first step was to eliminate all foods except small amounts of milk or one of its prepared forms such as koumiss, a beverage made from fermented mare's or camel's milk. As Mitchell's Philadelphia colleague Francis Dercum explained:

my own habit is never to ask a patient the question, "Does milk agree with you?" I simply order it. I am careful, however, to order it in small quantities, beginning with about 4 ounces every two hours and excluding absolutely all other food. This amount is of course insufficient for the needs of the body. I now find, that even if a disgust for milk is present the patient being placed upon a very small amount of food and becoming in a day or two very hungry becomes extremely grateful for the milk and takes it eagerly. My habit is next to increase the milk very slowly, being careful at first to keep my patient a little hungry all of the time. Finally in the course of a week or ten days, I increase the amount to 8, 10, or even 12 ounces every two hours, as the case may be. If I find that the patient is quite hungry by the fourth or fifth day I add a small slice of stale bread with butter once or twice a day. This I finally permit the patient to have three times daily. The diet is then further increased by a soft-boiled egg, or perhaps by a mere fraction thereof at breakfast. Finally a small chop or steak is given at noon, and a small quantity of thoroughly boiled rice may be given for supper. Upon these beginnings a substantial diet is finally built up, until the patient eats three large meals a day, such for instance as a breakfast of fruit, cracked wheat, one or two soft-boiled eggs, or a good sized steak or several chops, bread and butter, and milk; a dinner of a good slice of roast beef with vegetables and boiled rice (in place of potatoes) for dinner. The supper I prefer leaving as a light meal of bread, butter, fruits, light pudding, and milk.[7]

The patient was made to depend totally on the physician for all essentials of living; when the doctor told her that she would improve, she had no choice but to obey or die—from boredom if nothing else. The rest cure, therefore, like most other treatments for neurasthenia, depended in large part on the "personality of the physician." This phrase appears frequently in the literature on neurasthenia, and physicians emphasized that the doctor must not only have a good understanding of human nature but must also be able to use this understanding boldly. He must make the patient feel that he knew exactly what to do and was confident of improvement if the patient was faithful in following all instructions.

A crucial element of the rest cure was the demonstration of the physician's control. This was accomplished not only by his own management of the case but by the actions of his principal assistant—the trained nurse who attended the patient constantly and who was responsible for enforcing the doctor's orders. J. Madison Taylor, one of Mitchell's Philadelphia colleagues who had worked in Mitchell's clinic, explained why much care was needed in selecting a nurse who could carry out the physician's orders and use her own judgment when necessary: "Not only must she qualify technically, but intellectually, and in that far higher sphere which is inexactly described as the realm of the common sense, since it is one of the rarest of gifts. Her business is to maintain a symmetrical, consistent, daily routine, and keep the patient all the time busy 'guessing,' supplying just enough conversation, but not too much information or explanation. Patients often remark that the rest treatment was among the busiest periods of their lives. All this keeping busy is essential. The patient is, and should be, passive; in extreme cases absolutely so, all 'doings' being performed by others. At first the nurse actually places food in the recipient's mouth. Conversation had best be of the simplest. Part, and not the least part, of the cure," Taylor emphasized, "is the selection of the topics; the character of their pursuit is the duty of the nurse under hints supplied by the physician. I remember Dr. Mitchell once telling me a most significant incident. The patient was the daughter of a Catholic physician, who stipulated the nurse should be a devout Romanist. Whereupon I was directed to install a pink-cheeked Presbyterian. Old lines of thought need to be firmly set aside and new points of view presented. Suggestive education is paramount. In this the nurse is the constant, if not the chief, agent."[8]

In "The Yellow Wallpaper" Gilman graphically describes the torment of a woman kept from the creative writing that is her only link with the world and suffocated by the condescending attentions of her husband and brother, both physicians. The protagonist writes that

John is a physician and *perhaps*—(I would not say it to a living soul, of course, but this is a dead paper and a great relief to my mind)—*perhaps* that is one reason I do not get well faster.

You see, he does not believe that I am sick! And what can one do?

If a physician of high standing, and one's own husband, assures friends and relatives that there is really nothing the matter with one but temporary nervous depression—a slight hysterical tendency—what is one to do?

My brother is also a physician, and also of high standing, and he says the same thing.[9]

Clearly the male physician/female patient relationship provided doctors with many opportunities to exercise chauvinistic tendencies, and the possibilities for abuse of power were magnified by the nature of neurasthenia and of the rest cure.

Gilman later wrote a short piece entitled "Why I Wrote 'The Yellow Wallpaper,'" in which she told directly of her experience with the rest cure: "For many years I suffered from a severe and continuous nervous breakdown tending to melancholia—and beyond." In despair Gilman went to "a noted specialist in nervous diseases, the best known in the country. This wise man put me to bed and applied the rest cure, to which a still-good physique responded so promptly that he concluded there was nothing much the matter with me, and sent me home with solemn advice . . . 'never to touch pen, brush or pencil again' as long as I lived." Gilman tried to comply, and "came so near the borderline of utter mental ruin that I could see over."[10] Gilman concluded by claiming that this "great specialist later admitted to having modified the rest cure as a result of reading 'The Yellow Wallpaper,'" but, according to Suzanne Poirier, there is no evidence that Mitchell ever did so.[11]

The Weir Mitchell treatment—designed to last six to eight weeks—obviously required that a patient be both pliant and wealthy. There were many who did not meet these qualifications— notably men and those of moderate means—and physicians frequently modified Mitchell's treatment to satisfy the situation at hand. Irwin Neff, assistant superintendent of the Eastern Michigan Asylum for the Insane, outlined the essentials of the modified Weir Mitchell treatment in 1905. Noting that expense and the difficulty of finding adequately trained nurses made it impossible for many to undergo the full treatment, Neff commented that "the partial rest cure requires no special apparatus, no hospital care is needed; and the patient is his own nurse, the physician being his friend and advisor." Neff proposed a three-part treatment: first, the physician should take control of the patient's life; second, he should regulate the diet; and third, he should insure proper elimination through hydriatic techniques. Neff stated that "I am satisfied that the . . . [partial rest cure] will be of material assistance in the treatment of the many nervous cases which he [the physician] encounters." [12] The independent neurologist Lincoln Gray Taylor of Kansas City, Missouri, reported in 1907 that he had simply commanded a woman suffering from years of overwork and responsibility: " 'Young woman, you must go to bed for six weeks. Four of those weeks to be spent in bed, the remaining two from bed to chair and from chair back to bed.' At the end of that time you must go away on a visit for six months, then you will be quite well. All of which was duly carried out and she came home perfectly well." [13]

Men, who could not be as easily controlled as women and who furthermore often needed to maintain their business activities, were usually prescribed a modified rest cure. This required them to prolong the hours of rest in bed, to rise not earlier than nine or ten in the morning, and to retire in the early evening. As Dercum explained: "a man following this direction must necessarily curtail the hours devoted to work, and very often this simple expedient is sufficient to bring about a most favorable result." [14] As the neurologist Archibald Church of Chicago put it, even in severe cases "we cannot put [men] to bed with any expectation that they will stay there. I have tried it repeatedly and have nearly always failed. Men do not take to the recumbent position for any considerable length of time with equanimity. The fact of their being in bed constitutes an aggravation; and irritation is what we wish to exclude." [15]

Thus most physicians prescribing the rest cure for men modified it for their necessarily busier schedule; like the neurologist Landon Carter Gray, they allowed their male patients to continue with their work, provided they went "to and from their place of business in a carriage, passing from the carriage to bed." [16] Rest was a physiologically sound therapy, fitting well with the theory of overwork as a primary cause of neurasthenia and with Hodge's research demonstrating the changes that took place in nerve cells during fatigue. Rest had been less frequently prescribed than drugs during the 1870s, but by the 1880s it had become the treatment of choice for most physicians and remained so through 1910. The Weir Mitchell rest cure gained a respectable place among ANA members for their female patients, but most physicians employed a modified form of the rest treatment and encouraged their patients, both male and female, simply to divert their minds from themselves, to regulate their habits, and to get more sleep.

Sleep, like rest, enabled the patient to build up and store nerve force. Sleep was often induced through the use of hypnotics or sedatives such as chloral, trional, or bromides. According to Dr. George Morgan of Dover, New Hampshire, sleep was of such supreme importance that "when insomnia exists, sleep must be induced by artificial means. . . . It is through physiological sleep, where there is no opportunity for nervous discharge, that the nervous system achieves its highest degree of efficiency, and becomes possessed of an unusual quantity of potential energy. . . . I think it is much better to produce sleep by hypnotics than to allow the patient to lie awake night after night."[17] Though drugs steadily fell in favor from the 1870s, when they were the most frequently prescribed therapy, to the 1900s when they occupied fourth place, the neurasthenic pharmacopeia was extensive. By the turn of the century it had become customary for physicians to criticize those who relied too heavily on drugs in the treatment of neurasthenia, only to turn to a discussion of the ones they themselves usually employed.

The drug most frequently prescribed for the neurasthenic was strychnine or its derivative nux vomica. Though this poison has no therapeutic use today and can produce side effects including convulsions, muscle spasms, coma, and death, strychnine was used in small doses to stimulate the central nervous system. Presumably this stimulation removed all grounds for the common complaint of "lack of vitality." Other commonly used drugs included the "tonics and fortifiers" popular in patent medicines, which served nineteenth-century physicians well in a wide variety of ways. These preparations frequently included iron to build up the blood, arsenic—an "alterative"—and phosphates, which, like strychnine, acted as central nervous system stimulants. Both arsenic and phosphorous are poisons which accumulate in the body, and it is impossible to estimate the damage that their continued use must have caused, but few physicians resisted the temptation to prescribe some medication for stimulation, elimination, or improving sleep. Cannabis indica, a hemp preparation, was used both as a stimulant and anodyne or pain killer. Belladonna (atropine) and ergot—primarily utilized to relieve neurasthenic headache—had similar uses, though both also produced unpleasant side effects including nausea, vomiting, and convulsions. Stimulants such as caffeine acted to relieve constipation, as did the powerful purgative calomel, a staple of nineteenth-century therapeutics. These had the desired effect of regulating elimination—an important goal in treating the sluggish neurasthenic patient—and restoring mental and physical balance to the distressed system.

John V. Shoemaker, the noted professor of materia medica and president of the Medico-Chirurgical College of Philadelphia, expressed some of the ambivalence surrounding the use of medicinals in the treatment of neurasthenia in a 1903 clinical lecture. "Drugs," he maintained,

> are of less value than these methods of hygienic or physiological treatment. . . . Cold rubs and wet packs do good by rousing the activity of the circulation, increasing nervous energy, and promoting sleep, which is often fitful and broken in this disease. Such means are decidedly preferable to the use of coal-tar products, hypnotics, and sedatives. Although these are largely employed and sometimes accomplish temporary good, yet they are of no permanent avail, and, in fact, are capable of doing injury. Nor is it wise to be continually dosing the patient with medicines. The effect may be to cause additional impairment of an already weakened digestion or to establish a drug habit; in either instance the patient's condition will be worse than the first state.

Yet after citing these misgivings, Shoemaker went on to instruct his listeners that if they did use drugs, they should be "of such character as to lend strength and support to the nervous system. Arsenic, phosphorus, iron, zinc, and sometimes an antispasmodic may do good in selected cases or at certain times."[18]

The one exception to the rule of avoiding primary reliance on drugs was in the treatment of poor patients who applied to city dispensaries for relief of nervous conditions. Cecil MacCoy, assistant neurologist to the Brooklyn Dispensary operated by Arthur Conklin Brush (like MacCoy an independent neurologist), described the difficulties of treating poor neurasthenics in 1903. "Every case cannot be treated in the same way," he wrote, "but the same general principles must prevail. In a large dispensary service for nervous diseases one always sees patients with neurasthenia for whom the treatment must be almost entirely by drugs."[19] But even in these patients much care was given to the psychological, if necessarily cursory, management of the case. MacCoy noted that the first step was "questioning the new patient in regard to his sickness, its duration, probable cause, general symptoms, etc., and noting the same in the history book. . . ." Having made a diagnosis of neurasthenia, the physician should assure the patient that recovery was likely provided the sufferer followed instructions completely. The doctor then explained "the value of fresh air, sunlight, pure drinking water, the necessity of a daily sponge bath, and the action of the medicine [given] him. . . ." The drug of choice at Brush's clinic, MacCoy reported, was the bromide "given in 10 to 15 grain doses together with a few drops of Fowler's solution [potassium arsenite] in plenty of water after meals." But even if patients showed improvement immediately, they should be told that they must come to the clinic "for weeks, possibly months . . . [because the] slow and necessarily tedious education . . . plays a more important part in the treatment than is generally believed."[20] While dispensary physicians necessarily kept interviews short, then, they tried to emulate the therapeutic model set by private practitioners for middle-class and wealthy patients. As Frank R. Hallock, an ANA member from Cromwell, Connecticut, wrote in 1910, "the general principles underlying home, sanatorium and institutional treatment of neurasthenia and the psychoneuroses are essentially the same. The variations in the therapeutic procedure which may be attributed to residential conditions do not imply a change of these principles, but merely a difference in their application."[21] Hallock proposed founding psychopathic departments in city hospitals to accommodate the nervous poor and middle-class patients who could not afford private sanitariums.

Lacking proper facilities for the treatment of the poor, doctors used the means at hand to relieve immediate symptoms and tried to educate patients to healthy habits in what little time they could give them. Bernard Sachs, demonstrating clinic cases at the New York Polyclinic in 1891, advocated cold sponge baths, nutritious high-protein food, rest or diversion as the case required, and "above all . . . tonics [including] two drugs of the greatest importance,— first, strychnine, and, secondly, phosphorous."[22] Wharton Sinkler, a Philadelphia neurologist, in 1902 recommended phosphorous "in small doses" and arsenic "in moderate doses" for dispensary patients.[23] But as MacCoy explained, physicians could exploit the psychic effects of drug treatment more readily with poor patients than with the rich, who were likely to be more demanding of their doctors: "The patient's confidence, which is often so difficult to secure in the physician's private office, among the more well-to-do classes of neurasthenics, is often in the case of the dispensary classes, easily won. This is accomplished many times while the patient waits his turn on the benches outside the doctor's room, where old and new cases sit huddled together reciting to one another the marvelous benefits and cures made by the doctor."[24]

MacCoy recommended lukewarm sponge baths at night to induce sleep, hygienic lectures on food and drink, suggestion, and moral support. This support, which consisted of assuring patients each week that they were improved, looked better, and would soon be well, was the most important aspect of treatment, but as MacCoy observed, drugs must be used because they were expected and in fact demanded by the patient. "This order for medicine seems to be quite essential in the treatment of all classes of patients in the clinic or at the office, if you wish to hold your patient."[25]

While most physicians used drugs in treating neurasthenia, they often employed them more for their mental than physical effects. They especially criticized sole reliance on medicinals, as well as their too-frequent or careless administration. In 1905, Dr. William F. Waugh of Chicago warned against prescribing drugs for neurasthenia in a haphazard manner.

> No progress can be expected in the treatment of neurasthenia . . . as long as a group of remedies is gathered up and hurled at the victim in handfuls. Every case requires careful study . . . and the prescription of such remedies as are needed in that particular case, and of no others. Iron, quinine, arsenic, strychnine, phosphorus, manganese, lime, soda, potash, berberine, pepsin, pancreatin, papayotin, diastase, hydrochloric acid, phosphoric acid, and the rest of the tonics, may each be of value in its place, but by no stretch of the imagination can one conceive of all being needed in any one case at the same time; while the jumbling of all these together and firing the whole broadside into every case . . . seems archaic in the [twentieth] century.[26]

Another commonly prescribed treatment, which could be employed regardless of the patient's means and had less potential for harm than drugs, was exercise—though some physicians warned that exertion was the last thing needed by the neurasthenic's already overtaxed nervous system. Exercise improved appetite, elimination, and muscle tone while diverting the patient's mind from his troubles. Thus it was one of many treatments involving the principles of general good hygiene—fresh air, diet, change of scene—aimed at educating the patient to a more healthful lifestyle. Among the activities prescribed for neurasthenics were walking, bicycling, horseback riding, golf, and tennis, though at least one physician objected to the popular new pastime of automobiling—"a nerve exhausting method of taking exercise and diversion . . . [because] those who resort to this method of transportation and exercise usually show little judgment in regard to speed and keep themselves over exhilarated and in a state of nervous tension."[27] Bicycling and horseback riding were likewise contraindicated in sexual neurasthenia for reasons obvious to nineteenth-century physicians, who believed that stimulation of the genital area could produce sexual overexcitement.

Physical therapists such as John W. Bowler, director of the Dartmouth College gymnasium, and Watson L. Savage, who operated exercise clinics in New York and Pittsburgh, reported marked success in the treatment of neurasthenic cases by exercise. Both physicians took patients on referral. Savage, in a paper read before the Neurological Section of the New York Academy of Medicine in 1903, noted that he always sent his patients back to the original physician, and generally in much improved health. "Twenty years ago," he remarked proudly, "I came to this city and . . . announced to the medical profession my intention to use no medicine or drugs in my work, leaving that, when necessary, to the family physician. . . . It is a pleasure now for me to say I have lived up to this rule and in so doing have found the remedy exercise to have a wider field of usefulness year by year." [28]

Most physicians used exercise as an adjunct to other treatments and were careful to regulate its use in order to maintain control of the neurasthenic patient. The care shown in the prescription of exercise therapy—amount and types of exercise, time of day taken— exemplifies the profession's attempt to apply scientific methodology to diseases that were not scientifically understood. As more than one physician said, it was not the treatment per se but the way it was employed that made the difference in cases of functional nervous disorders. Thus physicians gave precise instructions that implied a more thorough knowledge of the disease than they actually possessed. While they frequently acknowledged this fact, they nevertheless used personal preferences and biases in devising elaborate therapeutic regimens. These prejudices sometimes resulted in ludicrously detailed prescriptions and proscriptions, but the advice doctors gave was based on their own observations of approaches that worked. The neurologist J. Harvey McBride, for example, cautioned that "outdoor walks should always be taken on the ground, never on pavements or verandas; the solid, unyielding character of a stone pavement is bad, and its unevenness of surface is worse, for the same muscles are brought into action at every successive step, and the repetition, like the movement of running a sewing-machine, is exhausting."[29] The use of explicit instructions also made it possible to assess in some measure the degree of cooperation displayed by the patient, a beneficial effect in itself and one that provided an indication of progress.

In cases of severe nervous prostration exercise was forgone in favor of such "passive" exercise regimens as massage, hydrotherapy, and electricity. These were employed when the patient was too weak to exercise or suffered from back pain or other symptoms that prohibited physical exertion. These therapies were also frequently used in conjunction with other treatments for their relaxing effect, calming the agitated mind and encouraging sleep. Water had a variety of therapeutic applications in the treatment of nervous patients, ranging from enemas to sponge baths, and, in cases of spinal tenderness, hot and cold packs to the spine. Robert E. Peck, an independent neurologist, explained in a lecture on neurology at the Yale Medical School in 1901 that hydrotherapeutic measures were useful in relieving the insomnia so persistent among neurasthenics. He particularly favored the wet pack, the cold rub, the hot full bath, and the "Neptune girdle." As he described it, the wet pack was applied by wrapping the patient in a coarse linen sheet wrung out of water at 60°F to 70°F. This was followed by wrapping the patient in several blankets. The cold rub was applied by throwing a linen sheet, wrung out of water at 60° to 70°F, quickly around the patient and then applying friction "by rapid passes of the hand." The Neptune girdle, Peck reported, "consists of a coarse linen bandage wide enough to cover the lower part of the trunk . . . and of sufficient length to pass around the body and overlap in front so as to provide a double thickness over the abdomen. This is wrung out of water at 60° to 75° F and covered with a dry bandage of either linen or flannel and pinned down snugly."[30]

Dr. James T. Whittaker of Cincinnati also endorsed hydrotherapy in conjunction with other treatments; he advised sponging patients off several times a day or having them "lie or sit enveloped in a wet sheet an hour or two every day."[31] An advantage of these treatments was that they could be applied by a member of the family if the patient could not afford a nurse; but as George W. McCaskey, a Fort Wayne gastroenterologist, observed, "the precise form and vigor of the hydriatic procedure must be regulated entirely by the clinical picture presented . . . which can only be learned by experimental observation." This of course meant that the physician must dictate the exact nature of the treatment. McCaskey reported that "a hot douche or spray of the entire body, from 110 to 120°F, . . . followed immediately by a cold douche at from 90 degrees in delicate patients, in the beginning of a course of treatment, down to 50 or less, have given me the best results."[32] Hydrotherapy was a relatively inexpensive treatment that could be performed even in the patient's home without a skilled therapist, thus making it affordable to large numbers of patients, but it still required the direct involvement of the physician. The number of baths, their duration, the temperature of the water—all were aspects of treatment requiring careful regulation by the physician. The patient was thus assured that the physician took an interest in his case, knew what to do about it, and was providing the most modern care available.

Electrotherapy was prescribed for neurasthenia far more often than hydrotherapy in the nineteenth century, though by 1910 its use had declined considerably. Several types of current—galvanic, faradic, and static—were used, frequently in combination, to stimulate the nervous system, improve elimination, and induce sleep. Galvanism, or galvanization, was a general treatment for the central nervous system. In this procedure, the seated patient held the negative pole at various points between the abdomen and the breastbone while the physician applied the positive electrode from the forehead to the top of the head and then down the entire length of the spine.[33] Faradization, producing a milder current, was used more specifically to affect various parts of the body. This procedure called for the seated patient's feet to rest on a copper plate attached to the negative pole while the physician applied the positive pole to the patient's body, often paying particular attention to the head and spine. The static current—franklinization—was produced when the "charged" patient, sitting on an insulated chair, was bombarded with sparks from a wind generator operated by the physician's assistant, while the physician moved a metal rod around the patient's body. Electrotherapy symbolized the profession's ability to incorporate modern technology into medical practice and satisfied the patient's demand that the doctor "do something." Its popularity was evidenced by the number of physicians who specialized as electrotherapists, or "electricians," but even a country doctor could afford to purchase a small apparatus.

As Dr. Francis B. Bishop explained to the tenth annual meeting of the American Electrotherapeutic Society in 1900:

> Massage, horseback-riding, bicycle-riding, walking, etc., are all good so far as they go, but they are all followed by fatigue, and these patients are already fatigued. They get up in the morning tired, and they go to bed tired. In electricity, however, we have a means of exercising not only the muscles of the body, but also the liver, the spleen, the kidneys, the stomach, and the intestines, and do all this in such a quiet gentle way as to be rather restful to the patient, and leave him invigorated instead of fatigued. It is my custom, . . . to begin by passing a very gentle galvanic current through the superior cervical ganglia, by placing a large pad over the solar plexus, or over the pit of the stomach, and, by a bifurcated cord, two small electrodes: one under each ear. This current, which should not be strong enough to produce uncomfortable dizziness, is allowed to pass for five minutes. Thus we gently stimulate the cells of the cortex cerebri and of the spinal cord, and through the pneumogastric we influence the stomach and intestines and increase their secretions, and, as the cells in the brain and spinal core are toned or gently stimulated, they are better prepared to transmit to the muscles and glands, when these are exercised or stimulated, that degree of healthy energy so necessary to enable them to functionate physiologically, and to produce those chemical changes so necessary to perfect nutrition.[34]

An advantage of electrotherapy was that, depending upon the placement of the electrodes, different parts of the body could be treated specifically; thus it was useful for various types of neurasthenia such as lithemic (sluggishness, with constipation), spinal, or cerebral. The neurologist Daniel Brower of Chicago, addressing the American Electrotherapeutic Society in 1900, defended the use of electricity against those who claimed that its effect was purely psychological. "Cerebral neurasthenia requires cerebral galvanization," he held.

> Some of the distinguished members of the profession do not accept the proposition that the brain is affected by galvanism, and insist that when results are obtained they are psychical, or purely suggestive. One of the surprising things of the times is the failure on the part of so many to appreciate the remedial power of this agent, the striking effects of which are so visible on every side as to entitle this to be called the electrical age. That the brain is affected by galvanism . . . may be demonstrated at any time by the vertigo, the forced movements, the cerebral malaise; the disturbance of consciousness, of sight, of taste, and of hearing; the vomiting, the pallor of the face, somnolence, and syncope which may follow cerebral galvanization.[35]

The therapeutic use of electricity, with its various strengths of currents and modes of application, called for skill and decision-making on the part of the physician. It was a powerful weapon in the hands of physicians who wished to keep their patients away from faith healers, mind curists, and self-help manuals; few patients would undertake to administer their own electrotherapy. Nevertheless, the use of electricity as a treatment for neurasthenia declined during the period, and it became more common for physicians who employed electrotherapy to justify its use on psychological grounds. As the Cincinnati neurologist Philip Zenner expressed it, "the moral influence . . . of electricity is very great. Almost invariably when I have applied both the static and some other form of electricity, faradism or galvanism, to a patient, he expressed himself as having special faith in the 'large machine,' and this element of faith is often a valuable one in treatment."[36]

Beard, though a pioneer in the medical uses of electricity, recognized the importance of the psychological or "mental therapeutics" in effecting the recovery of neurasthenic patients.[37] Creating "the expectancy of cure" was an important element of his treatment, and his published case records frequently note that "as usual, a favorable prognosis was given." In a controversial paper, "The Influence of the Mind in the Causation and Cure of Disease— The Potency of Definite Expectation," presented at the ANA's second annual meeting in 1876, Beard told the assembled members that disease could appear or disappear simply as a result of emotion.[38] He reported that he had told patients "that upon a certain day or hour, or even minute in some cases, they were to be better or be relieved of pain." These predictions, he asserted, set in motion a therapeutic force since "in ninety-nine cases out of a hundred, the emotions were supreme." Beard argued that the "effects which had been brought about through the emotions had been as permanent as those realized through the agency of medicines or electricity in the same class of patients," and that "the liability to disappointment in carrying out such therapeutics was no greater than that attending the use of any other remedial measure."

From the published remarks following Beard's presentation, the ensuing scene was lively, to say the least. Samuel G. Webber, William A. Hammond, and James Jackson Putnam charged that Beard was advocating deceit and humbuggery, and Hammond opposed publication of the paper in the ANA's transactions. Putnam regarded Beard's "experiments" as unscientific since the emotions could not be isolated and declared that he did not believe it proper "to state to our patients what we do not know positively." Webber charged that Beard had "approached very close to the border line between truth and deception" and that when "we overstepped the truth our profession was at once degraded." Hammond, clearly incensed, told the members that acceptance of Beard's ideas would make him feel like throwing his diploma away. He agreed that mental influence had sometimes produced results—noting particularly the water of Lourdes and the royal touch—but held that "if that form of practice was to be instituted, we should go back to monkery—give up our instruments, give up our medicines and enter a convent."

James Jewell, who had chaired the session, attempted to defend Beard, observing that "while this method of influencing our patients might be carried to excess" it was to be assumed that the honest physician would not do this. Jewell believed it to be "the wish of the author of the paper that the profession should candidly study the question, and endeavor to arrive at a golden mean in the application of this method of treatment." Beard, too, backed off and claimed that he had never argued for dispensing with other therapeutic measures but was simply encouraging physicians to practice suggestion more systematically.[39]

Not deterred for long, however, Beard returned to the ANA meeting the following year with another paper, entitled "Mental Therapeutics." Reiterating his toned-down position, he argued that all books on therapeutics should include a chapter on mental treatment. He concluded that "physicians of great scientific attainment and real worth, may fail when an obscure charlatan succeeds, because in the latter wonder and awe are excited, and these are more powerful therapeutically than simple respect." This time, Beard's views won more support among his colleagues. Edward Seguin regretted that he had not been able to participate in the discussions of the previous year—indicating how widely they must have been recounted—and sided with Beard on the role of emotion in therapeutics. Seguin maintained that doctors often employed methods that might be considered trickery by unsuspecting patients. He cited for example the use of hypnotics, "a very uncertain class of remedies," in which "we tell the patient, 'That will make you sleep,' and the hypnotic effect . . . [gives] the drug . . . a better chance to act. In many cases, the physician's conscience must be the higher law." Seguin's remarks were the only comments recorded after the reading of Beard's 1877 paper; thus general agreement with his more moderate view is indicated.[40]

Still, debate on the ethics of mental therapeutics and the question of how far such mental influence could go without becoming outright quackery continued at all levels of the medical profession. A discussion similar to that which had taken place at the ANA meetings of 1876 and 1877 occurred at a meeting of the Omaha Medical Society in 1891. At that meeting William F. Milroy, a

prominent local practitioner, read a short paper entitled "Neurasthenia Treated by the Keeley Method—A Case." Milroy described
the therapy used at a nearby clinic specializing in alcoholism and
drug addiction and asked the society's opinion on the ethics involved (though he had evidently decided that Keeley was a quack
and a threat to legitimate practitioners.)

Milroy reported that Dr. Keeley (a Rush graduate and formerly a
regular practitioner) relied almost entirely on hypodermic injec-
tions of placebos and guarantees of cure through positive thinking
and expectancy.[41] A number of commentators quickly pronounced
Keeley a fraud and his claim of using a secret remedy "not believed
for a moment by any intelligent practitioner." But others defended
Keeley on principle if "he cures where we fail." "If [he cures with]
chloride of gold," said one, "let us use chloride of gold." One doctor warned that if physicians could not oppose Keeley on scientific
grounds they would open themselves to charges of professional
jealousy from the public, and that "to the people at large it makes
no difference how they are cured so long as they are cured. . . ."
This physician summarized the profession's confusion over the use
of mental influence when he concluded, "I believe it is the laying on
of hands just as much as anything else, and I want to go on record
that it is my strong conviction that the Keeley cure is—well, what
it is I do not know, just as I do not know what the Christian Science cure is, but I see the beneficial effects in both cases, yet I believe it is a sort of laying on of hands, faith cure and humbug."[42]

Despite such ambivalence the emphasis on mental therapeutics
grew steadily throughout the period. The name of Freud was virtually unknown to the physicians who treated neurasthenia; two of
the seven authors citing his work before 1910 mistakenly referred
to him as "Freund" (apparently confusing him with the German
neurologist C. S. Freund), and the terms *psychoanalysis* or *psychotherapy* were used in only a handful of articles. But there was a
growing awareness of the mental aspects of neurasthenia and the
consequent indication that mental influences could be used successfully to treat it. The broad category of "mental therapeutics"
rose from seventh in popularity in the 1870s to third in the decades
between 1880 and 1910. Often the idea of mental suasion was

simply a perfunctory reference to the necessity of "gaining the patient's confidence," but many physicians elaborated on how this was to be accomplished. Among the methods frequently used were sympathy, suggestion, hypnotism, and, most important, "education of the patient"—pointing out the habitual errors that had produced illness and teaching a more wholesome lifestyle.

The first step in applying mental therapeutics was to perform a thorough physical examination and to question the patient in detail about his family background. Since the influence of heredity on nervousness was well known, this examination was already of recognized importance. As Dr. J. G. Biller of Cherokee, Iowa, explained in 1901, "this examination may or may not give us much information, but if it does not, it gives the patient confidence in us, or at least helps to do so, and this I consider a very important part of the treatment." "Do not think," he continued, "that I believe the only thing necessary to cure these people is faith; for, such is not the case; but a neurasthenic nervous system is lame, and in such a condition that it must have someone as a nervous crutch to help it along from time to time. . . ."[43]

Phrases such as "understanding the patient," "educating the patient," and "getting a firm mental grip on the patient" appear time and again in the neurasthenic literature. Physicians realized that nervousness was a condition that required careful and tactful management, perseverance, and often a lengthy period of treatment before the patient was well enough to function independently. As Theodore Fisher, a Boston alienist, said in 1872, "mental symptoms are as significant of nervous exhaustion as physical. . . . To get and keep the patient's confidence by exhibiting a critical knowledge of his case and a true sympathy for his sufferings . . . and to educate him out of his mistaken notions, requires more time and skill and patience than most physicians can afford to devote. . . ." Consequently the temptation was strong "to throw all such exaggerated ills into the wastebasket of disordered imagination, affronting the patient, and leaving him a prey to every form of quackery," but Fisher contended that the reward of seeing the patient's ultimate improvement was worth the effort required.[44]

Dr. H. C. Holbrook of Penacook, Maine, echoed Fisher's sentiment in 1876 when he commented that "in regard to the mental treatment something may be learned . . . from quacks, especially those belonging to the so-called Christian science and faith-cure systems. A secure mental grip on the patient may be the backbone of genuine professional success, as well as the mainstay and the whole stock in trade of charlatanry. What Beard calls the 'skill to manipulate the psyche of the patient' is, I believe, of the utmost importance. . . . [The] patient must be made to believe that you thoroughly understand his case and appreciate the suffering he endures; for if some psychical stimulus can be mingled with the administration of the remedies, their good effect will be much more marked."[45] Holbrook noted also that the neurasthenic's suffering was real and that "calling the patient a fool will not help much," though he added that "such a diagnosis is often the first one that presents itself to the mind of the physician."[46]

Dr. W. Blair Stewart of Atlantic City warned in 1901 of some of the mistakes an inexperienced physician could make in the treatment of neurasthenic patients and gave advice on the proper handling of such cases:

> Unless you gain the full confidence of your patient at the first visit your success will be endangered. Do not make your first examination and give an opinion until you have full time to go into every detail and make a thorough physical, mental, and antecedent study of the case. Do not speak doubtfully. Never tell your patient anything you cannot substantiate if questioned. . . . Never pass trivially over the patient's imaginary troubles, but give free attention to them on your first visit. Do not use the method of trying to shame away symptoms. Be sympathetic and attentive, but always firm, positive and strictly methodical. Do not allow yourself to show irritation by the patient's repetitions and questions. . . . Take time to sit by your patient and reassure in positive terms. Ten minutes quiet conversation will do much to relieve the worry, excitement, morbid fears and ideas, and mental depression. These talks must be given with the same regularity as medicine, and each visit will frequently show the mental effects produced by the

former. You must begin a system of mental education and start the mind moving along proper channels, and persist day by day until the power of your personality overbalances that of your patient.[47]

While he did not use the term psychotherapy, Stewart anticipated key elements of twentieth-century psychoanalysis, though he was clearly unaware of the problem of transference.

In 1895 James Jackson Putnam summarized the various methods of mental therapy that might be used in treating neurasthenia: first, those that helped the patient to exert his own will (reasoning, re-education) and second, those that operated without the direct intervention of the patient's will, such as hypnotism and suggestion. Though he preferred the first category because of its more permanent results, he believed that all had a place in treatment. Putnam concluded that "the principal good effect to be looked for from the psychical treatment of neurasthenia is . . . an improvement in hopefulness. . . . The seeds of hopefulness and confidence which are thus implanted so regulate the subconscious forces of the mind that the gain becomes steady and progressive."[48] As Frederick T. Simpson, an independent neurologist from Hartford, Connecticut, wrote in 1894, "it is very evident to anyone who consults the monographs and text-books of to-day, that there is no specific medicinal treatment for neurasthenia. All writers seem, however, to agree that much depends upon the personal qualities of the physician, or, as Putnam puts it, neurasthenic patients are cured, not by physics, but by the physician."[49]

Thus it is clear that physicians generally understood neurasthenia as a disease of the mind and mental therapy as an important aspect of treatment. The careful regimen imposed on the patient's daily life, even to the strict regulation of the diet, was a concept central to the goal of promoting a more wholesome mental outlook. Even the most apparently physical treatments such as electrotherapy and drugs were often prescribed for their psychic effect. These mental treatments did not employ such Freudian concepts as psychoanalysis or dream therapy—indeed, the goal of treatment was to divert the patient's mind from morbid preoccupation with self and to "avoid introspection." As the Cincinnati homeopath William Geohegan explained in a discussion of exercise, it "must be dissociated from one's vocation. If it keeps the mind busy so much the better as long as the wheels of thought are kept out of the well worn ruts."[50]

Images of ruts, channels, and paths appear regularly in pre-Freudian literature, based on the concept that repeated actions along certain nerve paths eventually made it unlikely that impulses would travel any other route, much like the process of feet wearing a path across a lawn.[51] Exercise "dissociated from one's vocation," changes of scenery, and new associations broke habitual patterns of behavior and provided a refreshing change. While neurologists promoted this hypothesis, it complemented physiological research and was a principle well known to physicians of all therapeutic persuasions. The chief criticism of the rest cure, therefore, was that it permitted the patient to dwell too much on self (though, according to Mitchell, this should be prevented by the nurse). While many physicians prescribed rest to shore up the depleted nerve force, then, they usually added other treatments aimed at encouraging a healthier mental framework. As the neurologist Graeme Hammond explained, "the feeding of the mind on self and the continual mental introspection . . . should be combated . . . [the goal of the treatment being] to divert the thoughts from morbid channels, stimulate the mental faculties in a normal direction and engender a feeling of brain rest and mental refreshment."[52]

The use of mental therapy cut across all specialty lines and was as likely to be employed by general practitioners in small towns as by well-known neurologists in big cities. While neurologists as a rule provided the most sophisticated arguments for "psychical treatment" and may have pioneered its use by that name, it is clear that physicians across the country recognized its value. Some of these "average" physicians singled out individual neurologists for praise as leaders in the field while others claimed they had been using such methods for years, but most recognized the value of mental therapy and took pains to incorporate its concepts into their own treatments. Some physicians, including a number of neurologists, continued to insist their treatment of choice had actual, rather than psychic effects, but the underlying emphasis on treatment of the mind itself grew as a theme in the neurasthenic literature throughout the period.

An excellent example of this shift in viewpoint is found in the use of travel as a treatment for neurasthenia. Beard believed that the cool, dry climate of the northeastern United States was a significant factor in the more frequent occurrence of neurasthenia in that part of the country.[53] He and others, therefore, often prescribed travel as a form of "climatotherapy" in which the nervous patient was sent to a more healthful environment to replenish his nerve stock. There was much debate in the literature as to which type of climate provided the best atmosphere, with authors alternately praising and condemning the mountains, seashore, ocean voyages, and trips to the Continent. With the growing emphasis on mental symptoms and psychic treatment of neurasthenia, climatotherapy declined in importance, but travel nevertheless increased as a prescribed treatment, moving from fourth place in the 1870s to second in the first decade of the new century.

The literature on travel reveals the medical profession's increasing awareness of the healthful mental effects of vacations, diversions, and changes of scenery, especially in cases of acquired neurasthenia resulting from stress. "Change is rest, in the majority of cases," said Dr. Shailer E. Lawton, president of the Vermont Medical Society, in 1900, "and now and then it becomes absolutely necessary for the patient to be removed from the associations and environments under which the neurasthenic condition developed. A sojourn among the hills and mountains, to those who are unaccustomed to such scenes, or a visit to the sea-shore to those unfamiliar with marine attractions, afford means for healthful diversion, while serving at the same time to lift the patient out of the old rut, and establish new and more agreeable combinations of thought. It also assists in breaking up pernicious habits and customs, and very frequently takes them away from the extremely injurious influence of emotional, over-sympathetic, and indiscreet relatives and friends."[54]

The Philadelphia neurologist Charles Mills attempted to promote the idea of two vacations per year for businessmen and for
women "whose manner of living calls for undue expenditure of
nervous force. . . ." One of these should be taken at the "usual"
time between the first of June and the first of October, while the
other should come, if possible, in February or March. "Physicians
and the community at large have come to recognize more and
more the importance of the summer vacation," Mills wrote, "but
the same is not true of the short vacation of late winter or early
spring. It is a well-known fact that nervous disorders are more numerous and more severe in the early weeks of spring. If the busy
man or woman could so arrange matters as to allow a holiday of
from two to three weeks late in February or early in March, in the
most congenial climate accessible, it would be found that this will
do almost as much in maintaining health and vigor as the usual
longer summer vacation." Lest his counsel appear to be based too
much on common sense and not enough on scientific medical
opinion, Mills added a few caveats on the principles of climatic
therapy: "For Americans north of the Maryland border, the Springs
of Virginia, or of North Carolina, the southern seaside resorts, the
Bermudas, Nassau, Cuba or Jamaica will be found desirable. . . .
Very high altitudes do not agree with neurasthenics, although they
may do well at resorts not higher than one to three thousand
feet." [55]

One independent neurologist, William Hutchinson of Providence, Rhode Island, carried the idea of travel therapy to the extreme by personally conducting his own tours. While his lecture
delivered to the Providence Medical Association in 1879 reads
more like a travelogue than a scientific report, it provides insight
into the aims of the travel cure. "For the last six years," he reported, "in company with a small number of patients—nerve invalids all—we have sought such lands as seemed best suited to our
needs, and in one instance only has the change of climate failed
to be of benefit." Citing the dictum "no news is good news,"
Hutchinson believed that the journey should be sufficiently long to
pass beyond the world of telegraph lines and business cables. Rul-

ing out European trips as too exhausting and the New England climate as too dry and changeable, he recommended various of the Caribbean islands in the Atlantic Ocean and the Sandwich Islands for those voyaging in the Pacific. Regarding "a good ship, attentive service, and first-class fare . . . [as] imperious necessities," Hutchinson went on to weigh the advantages and disadvantages of a number of stops on the Caribbean cruise. It is difficult to suppress a humorous mental image of Hutchinson shepherding his nervous charges as they steamed from port to port in search of the most restful and well-run establishment, but the doctor took his task quite seriously.

The Bermudas were disadvantaged by variable temperatures and high winds, Hutchinson thought. He considered the Bahamas most healthful and its principal city, Nassau, "remarkably good for a tropical colony." But its hotel, the Royal Victoria, was "ill-kept . . . and under the entire control of an utterly incompetent landlord." Martinique, by contrast, provided every comfort, and "[were] it not for one pest [the deadly fer-de-lance] I would give to Martinique the palm. . . . [But looking] back," Hutchinson concluded, "I must give the palm, so far as *we* are concerned, directly to the West Indies. Either Trinidad or Nassau for a stay, and the steamship trip for a shorter vacation."[56]

Unusual approaches to the treatment of neurasthenia seem to have been the particular province of independent neurologists. Some, like Hutchinson, elaborated on common themes of treatment, while others constructed their own appliances to administer unique therapies. Albert E. Sterne, an independent neurologist from Indianapolis who ran the Norways Sanitarium, for example, promoted the therapeutic use of the "primeval" actinic rays of sunlight. To this end he constructed a cabinet in which the nude patient sat with the head protruding into a sliding dome. Arc lamps utilizing vacuum conductors then generated actinic rays inside the cabinet while the head was bathed by air charged with ozone. "The results," Sterne reported, "have been almost uniformly excellent. A large number of cases have been treated during the past six years, and there have been few, if any, failures to report. This is especially true as regards the neurasthenic aches and pains along the spinal column and in other regions of the body. Not only have the individual results been good, but the duration of treatment has been materially lessened, in some cases fully one-half. This is clearly evidenced by a comparison of the period during which patients remained at the sanitarium before and since the inauguration of this method at 'Norways.'"[57]

J. Leonard Corning, an independent neurologist in New York City, pioneered the use of compressed air, theorizing that neurasthenics' faulty circulation could be improved by administering drugs in a condensed atmosphere. With the aid of an engineering firm Corning constructed a large metal chamber in his cellar, "able to withstand a pressure equal to that of a locomotive boiler," with a blow-off valve to prevent accidents. Using a one horsepower electric motor "actuated by the current derived from the street conduits of the Edison Electric Illuminating Company" and an elaborate system of switches, belts, and pulleys, Corning was able to achieve thirty pounds of pressure to the square inch. Patients were strapped to a chair inside the chamber and kept under pressure for up to two hours, then decompressed for twenty to thirty minutes during which time they self-administered a cardiac stimulant made up of "fifty or sixty drops of the aromatic spirits of ammonia to which caffeine, the sulphate of sparteine, or some other heart-tonic may be added. . . ."[58] Corning reported that a neurasthenic woman suffering from insomnia fell asleep during treatment and, "on the following day . . . [went] home, and . . . immediately [fell] asleep, only awaking after the lapse of five or six hours. I will merely add," said Corning, "that this case went on to complete recovery, natural sleep supervening regularly without artificial assistance of any kind. . . ."[59]

Exotic equipment like Corning's and Sterne's had much the same psychic effect as electrotherapeutic machinery, with the attraction of novelty added to the impressive harnessing of modern technology. Independent neurologists may have been particularly aggressive in inventing unusual devices for their competitive value against the ANA establishment, or possibly it was the use of such unorthodox appliances that blocked their admission to the ANA in the first place (though hardly any neurasthenic treatments seem more bizarre today than the electrotherapeutic gear). As Curran Pope, an independent neurologist from Louisville, explained in an address to his district medical society, "the physician must be the master of every move . . . [combining] a calm, judicious bearing, the inspiration of confidence, a thorough knowledge of every detail of the case, an intricate knowledge of human nature, the patience of Job . . . [and mastery of] every mechanical, electrical, and hydro-therapeutical appliance. . . ."[60] But all physicians agreed that combination therapy was the key to success in the management of neurasthenia.

By the early years of the twentieth century the American medical community was moving increasingly toward psychological treatment of subjective nervous disorders. Not yet aware of the work of Freud in Vienna, they nevertheless made use of the skills available to them and relied on their own understanding of human nature in their attempts to guide nervous patients back to health. For their role as leaders in this movement neurologists owed much to the work of George Beard. Beard, though usually guilty of exaggeration and oversimplification, made two important contributions to nineteenth-century psychiatry that outweighed his errors: first, he legitimized functional emotional imbalances by giving them a nonderogatory label, and second, he led the way toward psychological management of such cases by the regular medical profession. In sum, it was not his reasoning but his intuition that accounted for Beard's prominence in American neurology. As he commented in 1877, "in pathology, strictly speaking, nothing is imaginary. When we use the term imaginary in relation to disease; we mean subjective as distinguished from objective; but the former are as much realistic as the latter. A man who induces or maintains a state of disease through an excess of self-absorption by turning his mind upon himself through the emotions of fear and expectation, may be just as truly diseased as though he were knocked down with an axe."[61]

A common perception of the history of twentieth-century psychiatry is that Freud introduced psychiatric principles to a world dominated by physical views of disease and somatic treatments. Even medical historians have associated the beginnings of modern psychiatry in the United States primarily with the American Neurological Association, whose leaders were responsible for bringing Freud to America. The evidence of the medical journal literature on neurasthenia presents a quite different view. By the late 1800s there was a large and diverse community within the medical profession that was moving steadily toward psychiatric treatment of nervous disorders despite physicians' ignorance of Freudian concepts, which, in any case, were still largely unformed. The physicians who treated neurasthenia were well trained, if nonspecialized; they recognized mental symptoms in their neurasthenic patients, understood the reality of their suffering, and used the means at hand to help relieve their patients' unhappiness. Though they saw neurasthenia as a single disease rather than a number of loosely related symptoms, the attention they gave to specific symptomatology as well as to the overall emotional state of their patients indicates considerable insight into the mechanisms involved in producing nervous conditions. More important, they recognized the psychological dependence such patients had on their physicians and met this need by performing thorough examinations, taking case histories, prescribing detailed treatments that provided instructions for daily living, and acknowledging the necessity in many cases for long-term care.

While the ANA provided leadership in the recognition and psychological management of nervous complaints, its members by no means had a monopoly on practice. Their specialty was based on principles of intuition and insight, and in this sense they were in danger of being spoiled by their success. Neurologists could impress patients with their high-technology gadgetry and evidently could frequently effect marked improvement with a combination of educational techniques, common sense, and various persuasive measures, but they had little in their arsenal that general practitioners or even nonmedical healers could not also acquire with relative ease. While many neurologists professed fears of losing patients to quacks, the unmistakable evidence is that they were facing at least as great a challenge from within the ranks of their own profession. In fact, a number of neurologists contributed to this threat by educating nonspecialists to the psychic treatment of neurasthenia through lectures and medical articles. It was not until the 1920s that psychiatry emerged as a specialty distinct enough to prevent physicians not trained in psychiatry from adding mental treatments to their practices. The Freudian system of psychoanalysis, because it emphasized mental processes exclusively and required substantial investment of time and money in specialized training, was especially instrumental in ending the more holistic approach to health care that had been traditional in American medicine.

NOTES

1. George M. Beard, "Nervous Exhaustion (Neurasthenia) with Cases of Sexual Exhaustion," *Maryland Medical Journal,* 6 (1880), 294.

2. Francis X. Dercum, "The Treatment of Neurasthenia, with Special Reference to the Rest Cure," *Transactions of the Pan-American Medical Congress,* 1895, pt. 1, p. 470.

3. S. Weir Mitchell, "Neurasthenia, Hysteria, and Their Treatment," *Chicago Medical Gazette,* 1 (1880), 156.

4. Barbara Sicherman, "The Uses of a Diagnosis: Doctors, Patients, and Neurasthenia," *Journal of the History of Medicine,* 32 (1977), 50–51.

5. Sarah Stage, *Female Complaints: Lydia Pinkham and the Business of Women's Medicine* (New York: W. W. Norton & Co., Inc., 1979), p. 86.

6. See Charlotte Perkins Gilman, "The Yellow Wallpaper," in Ann J. Lane, ed., *The Charlotte Perkins Gilman Reader* (New York: Pantheon, 1980), pp. 3–19. Originally published in the January 1892 issue of the *New England Magazine.*

7. Dercum, "Treatment of Neurasthenia," p. 469.

8. J. Madison Taylor, "The Essence of the Rest Cure," *Monthly Cyclopedia and Medical Bulletin,* 1 (1908), 279-80.

9. Lane, *Gilman Reader,* pp. 3–4.

10. Ibid., pp. 33–34.

11. Suzanne Poirier, cited by Paula Treichler. Correspondence with Carole Appel, July 23, 1986.

12. Irwin Neff, "Pathological Fatigue and Its Treatment," *Physician and Surgeon,* 27 (1905), 206–7.

13. Lincoln Gray Taylor, "Some Unrecognized Forms of Neurasthenia," *Medical Brief,* 35 (1907), 358.

14. Dercum, "Treatment of Neurasthenia," p. 468.

15. Archibald Church, "Treatment of Neurasthenia," *Chicago Medical Recorder,* 20 (1901), 323.

16. Landon Carter Gray, "Neurasthenia: Its Differentiation and Treatment," *New York Medical Journal,* 48 (1888), 425.

17. George P. Morgan, "Neurasthenia," *Transactions of the Maine Medical Association,* 15 (1904), 175.

18. John V. Shoemaker, "Neurasthenia," *Medical Bulletin,* 25 (1903), 388–89.

19. Wharton Sinkler of Philadelphia used exactly the same wording in 1902. See Sinkler, "Treatment of Neurasthenia," *International Medical Magazine,* 11 (1902), 78.

20. Cecil MacCoy, "Some Observations on the Treatment of Neurasthenia at the Dispensary Clinic," *Brooklyn Medical Journal,* 17 (1903), 400–401.

21. Frank R. Hallock, "The Sanatorium Treatment of Neurasthenia and the Need of a Colony-Sanatorium for the Nervous Poor," *Yale Medical Journal,* 17 (1910–11), 136.

22. Bernard Sachs, "Functional Nervous Troubles: Neurasthenia, Its Occurrence in Young and Old, Symptomatology, and Treatment," *International Clinics,* 1 (1891), 241.

23. Sinkler, "Treatment of Neurasthenia," p. 80.

24. MacCoy, "Some Observations on the Treatment of Neurasthenia," p. 400.

25. Ibid., p. 401.

26. William F. Waugh, "Neurasthenia: Drug and Dietary Treatment," *Therapeutic Medicine,* 1 (1907), 66.

27. Charles K. Mills, "The Treatment of Neurasthenia," *Proceedings of the Philadelphia County Medical Society,* 26 (1905–6), 384.

28. Watson L. Savage, "Exercise in the Treatment of Neurasthenia," *Journal of Advanced Therapeutics,* 27 (1909), 515. See also John W. Bowler, "The Hygienic and Physical Exercise Treatment of Cardiac and Neurasthenic Cases," *New Albany Medical Herald,* 28 (1910), 49–52.

29. J. Harvey McBride, "Some Points in the Management of the Neurasthenic," *Transactions of the State Medical Society of Wisconsin,* 1901, p. 317.

30. Robert E. Peck, "The Medicinal and Hygienic Treatment of Neurasthenia," *Yale Medical Journal,* 7 (1900–1901), 425.

31. James T. Whittaker, "Neurasthenia," *International Medical Magazine,* 4 (1895–96), 722.

32. George W. McCaskey, "Neurasthenia: Some Points in Its Pathol-

ogy and Treatment," *Journal of the American Medical Association,* 34 (1900), 1534.

33. George M. Beard and A. D. Rockwell, *A Practical Treatise on the Medical and Surgical Uses of Electricity,* 6th ed. rev. (New York: William Wood & Company, Publishers, 1888), p. 376.

34. Francis B. Bishop, "The Cause of Some Cases of Neurasthenia, and Their Treatment by Electricity," *Transactions of the American Electrotherapeutic Society,* 1900, p. 331.

35. Daniel R. Brower, "Cerebral Neurasthenia, or Failure of Brain-Power, with Special Reference to Its Electro-Therapeutics," *Transactions of the American Electrotherapeutic Society,* 1900, p. 336.

36. Philip Zenner, "Treatment of 'Nervousness,'" *Cincinnati Lancet and Clinic,* 23 (1889), 491.

37. As Charles L. Dana recalled in 1923, "[Beard] believed in electricity, but when one day his battery did not work, he continued his applications with dead electrodes and discovered psychotherapeutics." Charles L. Dana, "Dr. George M. Beard: A Sketch of His Life and Character, with Some Personal Reminiscences," *Archives of Neurology and Psychiatry,* 10 (1923), 429.

38. Beard probably "lifted" much of his talk from the British alienist Hack Tuke's text on psychotherapy. Nathan Hale, Jr., *Freud and the Americans: The Beginnings of Psychoanalysis in the United States, 1876–1917* (New York: Oxford University Press, 1971), pp. 65–66.

39. George M. Beard, "The Influence of the Mind in the Causation and Cure of Disease—The Potency of Definite Expectation," *Journal of Nervous and Mental Disease,* 3 (1876), 429–36.

40. George M. Beard, "Mental Therapeutics," *Journal of Nervous and Mental Disease,* 4 (1877), 581–82.

41. See H. Wayne Morgan, *Drugs in America: A Social History, 1800–1980* (Syracuse: Syracuse University Press, 1981), pp. 74–83, for more on Keeley.

42. William F. Milroy, "Neurasthenia Treated by the Keeley Method—A Case," *Omaha Clinic,* 4 (1891), 206–19.

43. J. G. Biller, "Treatment of Neurasthenia," *Journal of the American Medical Association,* 38 (1902), 4.

44. Theodore W. Fisher, "Neurasthenia," *Boston Medical and Surgical Journal,* 86 (1872), 72.

45. H. C. Holbrook, "Dissertation on Certain Forms of Nerve Weakness," *Transactions of the New Hampshire Medical Society,* 1886, pp. 96–97.

46. Ibid., p. 93.

47. W. Blair Stewart, "The Treatment of Neurasthenia," *Transactions of the Medical Society of New Jersey,* 1901, pp. 189–90.

48. James Jackson Putnam, "Remarks on the Psychical Treatment of Neurasthenia," *Boston Medical and Surgical Journal,* 132 (1895), 511.

49. Frederick T. Simpson, "Acquired Cerebral Neurasthenia," *Yale Medical Journal,* 1 (1894–95), 114.

50. William A. Geohegan, "Neurasthenia," *The Clinique,* 23 (1902), 700.

51. Charles E. Rosenberg, *The Trial of the Assassin Guiteau: Psychiatry and Law in the Gilded Age* (Chicago: University of Chicago Press, 1968), pp. 58–59.

52. Graeme M. Hammond, "The Bicycle in the Treatment of Nervous Diseases," *Journal of Nervous and Mental Disease,* 19 (1892), 37.

53. A brief discussion of the idea that meteorological conditions played an important role in designing therapeutic regimes for individual patients (the principle of specificity) is contained in John Harley Warner, *The Therapeutic Perspective: Medical Practice, Knowledge, and Identity in America, 1820–1885* (Cambridge: Harvard University Press, 1986), pp. 58–80.

54. Shailer E. Lawton, "Neurasthenia," *Transactions of the Vermont Medical Society,* 1900, pp. 49–50.

55. Mills, "Treatment of Neurasthenia," p. 388.

56. William F. Hutchinson, "Climate Cure in Nervous Diseases," *Medical Record,* 17 (1880), 3–6.

57. Albert E. Sterne, "Neurasthenia and Its Treatment by Actinic Rays," *Journal of the American Medical Association,* 42 (1904), 505.

58. J. Leonard Corning, "The Use of Compressed Air in Conjunction with Medicinal Solutions in the Treatment of Nervous and Mental Affections," *Medical Record,* 40 (1891), 229.

59. Ibid., p. 231.

60. Curran Pope, "The Value of Certain Therapeutics in Functional and Organic Nervous Diseases," *Atlanta Medical and Surgical Journal,* 13 (1896–97), 743.

61. George M. Beard, "The Nature and Treatment of Neurasthenia (Nervous Exhaustion), Hysteria, Spinal Irritation, and Allied Neuroses," *Medical Record,* 12 (1877), 583.

FIVE

The Pre-Freudians

Most historical views of neurasthenia have been gleaned from the writings of elite neurologists in major cities who contributed the theoretical basis of understanding of the disease and who were recognized as authorities on the management of nervousness. This literature provides information on the intellectual development of the concept of neurasthenia, but it has led to the misperception that the disease was of concern to only a few medical practitioners. Historians who have touched on neurasthenia have described it as a faddish disease afflicting the upwardly mobile middle class, who aspired to "nervous exhaustion" as a social distinction, much as Americans in the mid-twentieth century popularized the "nervous breakdown." In reality, as we have seen in preceding chapters, neurasthenia was recognized and treated by physicians throughout the late nineteenth-century medical community. This observation demonstrates not only the prevalence of nervous diseases in the period but also the concern which these disorders created. Far from ignoring or scorning the victims of nervousness, physicians of a variety of specialties showed compassion for such patients and undertook their treatment. The journal literature indicates that most physicians did not refer nervous patients to neurologists, but took it upon themselves to learn as much as possible about the disease in order to achieve their goal of treating the "whole patient."

An analysis of the doctors who contributed to the neurasthenic literature sketches the background of several important themes: the "trickling" of ideas through the medical community, the reverse flow of grass-roots opinion in shaping medical theory and practice, and the state of specialization and professional competition in nineteenth-century American medicine. There were no scientific breakthroughs in this era to influence psychiatric theory or practice. Physicians relied on empirical observations, their understanding of human nature and their own mental processes, and the social mores of the culture in which they lived to form theoretical models of mental disorders. These philosophies, though "unscientific," were arrived at by the same processes employed by twentieth-century psychiatrists including Freud, Jung, Adler, and Horney. Because a theoretician of Freud's stature had not yet emerged, a relative democracy existed among those concerned with mental health and illness. Even lay practitioners like Christian Scientists and mind curists played a significant role in psychological therapy, and a diverse group of physicians within the regular medical profession contributed to the body of scientific knowledge on nervousness.

Most American physicians who wrote on the subject of neurasthenia published their reports in the medical journals that were becoming important channels of professional communication and that represented the most advanced scientific dialogue at the time. The physicians who wrote on neurasthenia present a cross-section of the medical profession not only as it perceived neurasthenia but also, because of the subjective and amorphous nature of the disease, as it viewed concepts of mental health, correct living, and treatment of emotional disorders in general.

A few physicians, like George Beard and Charles Dana, were noted authorities on disorders of the nervous system. But only forty-six, or less than 20 percent of the medical journal authors, were neurologists who were also members of the prestigious ANA, although this group did produce proportionately more of the literature on the disease, contributing almost one-quarter (eighty-one) of the 332 articles analyzed for the present study. A second group of thirty-two physicians, or slightly over 12 percent of the authors, identified themselves as neurologists but were not affiliated with the ANA. This group wrote 14 percent (forty-seven) of the articles on neurasthenia. The reasons for the independent status of these physicians are not entirely clear. Since the ANA required election to membership and, in fact, placed a limit on membership, we can assume that some of these physicians may have been excluded because of personal conflicts or disputes over professional qualifications, while others may simply have chosen not to apply.

Even more striking than the presence of these independent neurologists is the contribution of a large group of physicians who wrote on neurasthenia but were not neurologists of any kind. The existence of this latter body of doctors who wrote more than half of the journal literature on the disease has been unrecognized by historians. The focus on medical leadership in tracing the intellectual development of scientific ideas has obscured the role of these physicians who wrote much of the literature on neurasthenia and who helped to shape the American medical community's response to psychological problems both before and after the introduction of Freudian concepts. This group included gynecologists, alienists, general practitioners, oculists, dentists, electrotherapists, surgeons, pharmacologists, and other practitioners. These 184 physicians wrote 204 (61 percent) of the articles on neurasthenia. Thus, they were more likely to contribute a single article than were members of either of the other groups. The part they played in treating nervous disorders before the days of the specially trained psychiatrist provides insight into some of the conflicts that have long existed between the holistic view of health care and medical specialization. The fact that the majority of the articles on neurasthenia were written by nonspecialists should not be particularly surprising in light of the lack of differentiation in professional ranks at the time. Specialty boards did not become common until after World War I, and until formal training separated specialists from nonspecialists in the field of psychiatry, most physicians felt themselves capable of treating patients with nervous and mental diseases.

Table 4. Physician Groups

	N	Percent of Total
American Neurological Association	46	18
Independent Neurologists	32	12
Non-Neurologists	184	70
	262	100

The physicians who wrote on neurasthenia were overwhelmingly male (there were only six women in the entire group) and married, a pattern consistent with other professional groups of the period. Nearly all (94 percent) were "regulars," meaning that they subscribed to the traditional therapeutics taught in the majority of medical colleges and supported by the American Medical Association (AMA). Eleven were homeopaths, four were eclectics, and three were of unknown therapeutic persuasion (this at a time when approximately one-fifth of the practitioners in the nation were irregulars).[1] The high degree of professional involvement among the authors suggests that as a whole they were elite among their colleagues, a premise supported by the simple fact that they did publish in a medical journal. Fully two-thirds, or 136 of the 209 physicians for whom membership information was obtained, were members of the AMA, and 183, or almost 90 percent, also belonged to their local and state medical societies—an unusually high figure given the fact that dual membership was not required and that many AMA members chose not to join their local societies. Thus, even the less well known physicians tended to be professionally active and may have been prominent in their communities, though they received no national acclaim.

There is little doubt that the neurologists who were members of the American Neurological Association were the recognized authorities on the subject of neurasthenia and enjoyed the highest professional status of the three groups. Thirty-seven percent of the doctors in this group were in the highest status bracket (listed in one or more medical biographical dictionaries), while 16 percent of the independent neurologists and only 14 percent of the non-neurologists were. An additional 47 percent of the ANA members were listed in *Who Was Who* only, as were 26 percent of the independent neurologists and 18 percent of the non-neurologists.

The typical ANA member in 1900 was born in the Northeast in the 1850s. He attended a good medical school such as the University of Pennsylvania or the College of Physicians and Surgeons of New York, graduated in the 1880s, and received his license to practice soon after.[2] To supplement his education he did postgraduate work in Europe, where the quality of medical education was considered superior to that generally available in the United States. After a year or two abroad, during which time he visited the laboratories and clinics of leading Continental researchers and perhaps earned a certificate of attendance, he returned to open a private neurological practice in a major city on the East Coast.[3] At one time or another he would maintain an affiliation with a public hospital (a badge of distinction), a private sanitarium, or an asylum as a consulting or attending neurologist. Often the hospital was the teaching component of a medical school with which he held a faculty position. If this were the case, the professorial position was likely to be with a high-quality institution comparable to the one he had attended as a medical student. Men like George Beard, A. D. Rockwell, Weir Mitchell, Charles Dana and Francis Dercum each represented the typical neurologist to a great extent, exhibiting only minor personal variations and demonstrating the overall cohesiveness of this select group.

George Miller Beard, for example, was born in the hamlet of Montville, Connecticut, in 1839, the son of a Congregational minister and grandson of a physician. He completed his preparatory education at Phillips Andover Academy, taught school briefly, and graduated from Yale in 1862. From his seventeenth to his twenty-third year, Beard suffered from many of the symptoms he was later to recognize in his patients—ringing in the ears, pains in the side, dyspepsia, nervousness, morbid fears, and "lack of vitality." Perhaps because of his own experience with the disease, Beard believed that neurasthenia was commonly an illness of young adulthood that often disappeared between the ages of twenty-five and thirty-five. Beard's suffering seems to have been prompted largely by his doubts

Table 5. Distribution of Physicians by Residence Type (1900 Population)

Population	American Neurological Association Percent	N	Independent Neurologists Percent	N	Non-Neurologists Percent	N	Total Percent	N
Over 500,000	71.7	(33)	31.2	(10)	27.1	(49)	35.5	(92)
250,000–500,000	8.7	(4)	15.6	(5)	16.0	(29)	14.7	(38)
100,000–250,000	8.7	(4)	25.0	(8)	10.0	(18)	11.5	(30)
25,000–100,000	2.2	(1)	9.4	(3)	11.0	(20)	9.3	(24)
Under 25,000	8.7	(4)	18.8	(6)	35.9	(65)	29.0	(75)
	100.0	(46)	100.0	(32)	100.0	(181)	100.0	(259)

Significance = .000   Gamma = .479

Source: Study Data

Table 6. Physician Groups by Medical School Classification

School Classification	American Neurological Association Percent	N	Independent Neurologists Percent	N	Non-Neurologists Percent	N	Total Percent	N
Class A	61.9	(26)	56.0	(14)	51.9	(81)	54.3	(121)
Class B	35.7	(15)	28.0	(7)	32.7	(51)	32.7	(73)
Class C	2.4	(1)	16.0	(4)	15.4	(24)	13.0	(29)
	100.0	(42)	100.0	(25)	100.0	(156)	100.0	(223)

Significance = .248   Gamma = .183

Source: "Third Classification of Medical Colleges of the United States," *Journal of the American Medical Association*, 60 (1913), 231–34.

regarding choice of a career and perhaps guilt over his lack of religious commitment—common causes of stress in the young. Two brothers followed his father into the ministry, and Beard chastised himself in his journal for his indifference to spiritual concerns. He also had a taste for champagne and tobacco, pleasures forbidden in his father's austere household. Apparently his decision to become a physician cured him of his doubts and he never suffered again from the distresses of his youth but entered medicine with a sense of mission to help others similarly afflicted.[4] He entered Yale Medical College in 1862 and, after a brief interruption to serve in the U.S. Navy during the Civil War, transferred to the College of

Physicians and Surgeons of New York and earned his medical degree in 1866. He married in the same year and settled permanently in New York City.

Beard became fascinated early on by the medical uses of electricity, an interest shared by his colleague, A. D. Rockwell. The two founded the Electrotherapeutical Society in 1871 and wrote some of the earliest works in the field of electrotherapeutics, including *A Practical Treatise on the Medical and Surgical Uses of Electricity,* first published in 1871. In 1874 Beard founded the *Archives of Electrology and Neurology,* though this journal survived only two years. Beard wrote prolifically on a host of psychological topics including trance, hypnotism, and inebriety, in addition to neurasthenia. Many of his articles were published in magazines such as the *Popular Science Monthly,* and he was a frequent public lecturer. He was extremely active professionally, belonging to numerous medical societies and holding a faculty position as lecturer on nervous diseases at New York University. He also served as physician for electrotherapeutics and nervous diseases at the Dewitt Dispensary from 1873 to 1876, and was a delegate to the International Medical Conference in London in 1881.

Beard was representative of the founding generation of ANA members. He was urbane, professionally active, and showed no hesitation in using the prestige of his position to influence public opinion. He was outspoken in arguing for the acquittal of Guiteau on the basis of insanity and appeared before President Arthur as a representative of the National Association for the Protection of the Insane to plead for a commission to investigate Guiteau's mental state.[5] Beard was a prolific writer, but his work was criticized by younger neurologists as being overly philosophical, bombastic, and poorly researched.[6]

Beard's colleague and partner Alphonso David Rockwell, also among the older members of the ANA, remained philosophically aligned with Beard though he outlived his more famous collaborator by fifty years. Rockwell invited Beard into partnership in 1868, and the two maintained their association until 1874, when Beard terminated it to devote more time to writing and lecturing.[7] Rockwell was professor of electrotherapeutics at the New York

Post-Graduate School of Medicine from 1888 to 1892 and was neurologist and electrotherapist to the Flushing Hospital from 1904 until his retirement from active practice in 1912. It was his association with Beard, however, that did most to establish Rockwell's reputation. Their textbook on electrotherapeutics went into nine editions, and Rockwell completed the manuscript on sexual neurasthenia that Beard was working on at the time of his death.

Both Beard and Rockwell were members of the New York Neurological Society, one of four metropolitan societies affiliated with the ANA (including those at Philadelphia and Chicago, and a second New York association in Brooklyn). Other members of the large New York Association included Charles Loomis Dana, who worked briefly with Beard; European-trained Bernard Sachs; Joseph Collins, a New York University graduate with extensive clinical experience; Landon Carter Gray, a Bellevue graduate who served a term as president of the ANA; and Moses Allen Starr, a long-time faculty member at Columbia University.

The Philadelphia Neurological Society, founded in 1883 by Charles Mills and Francis Dercum, was by far the most inbred of the local ANA subsidiaries. The Philadelphia group included a number of aristocratic and influential neurologists who were mostly born and raised in that city and whose names were among the most prominent in the neurological specialty. The membership included Weir Mitchell and his son John Kearsley Mitchell, Wharton Sinkler, Charles W. Burr, Horatio C. Wood, and Daniel J. M'Carthy. All were faculty or trustees of either Jefferson Medical College or the University of Pennsylvania, and all except the younger Mitchell served terms as president of the ANA.

Members of the smaller Chicago ANA society included James S. Jewell, a founding member of the ANA and its first president from 1875 to 1879, and cofounder and editor of the *Journal of Nervous and Mental Disease;* Harold N. Moyer, a Rush graduate who did postgraduate work in Europe; and Hugh Patrick, president of the ANA in 1907 and twice president of the local chapter.

Other ANA contributors to the neurasthenic literature included Robert T. Edes, who took his M.D. from Harvard in 1861 and served on the Harvard faculty; James Jackson Putnam, another member of the Harvard faculty, perhaps best known as one of the earliest converts to Freudian psychoanalysis in the United States; and Edward Cowles, an 1863 graduate of both Dartmouth and the College of Physicians and Surgeons of New York, who ran the McClean Hospital for the insane and taught at Dartmouth and Harvard. It is evident that the early members of the American Neurological Association had much in common with one another. Most knew others in the association before joining themselves, through either city of residence or medical school. The single most important predictor of ANA affiliation among neurologists was city of residence; 72 percent of ANA members lived in cities over 500,000 while only 31 percent of independent neurologists lived in major cities. ANA members were somewhat older than the average neurologist who did not affiliate with the ANA before 1910, and they remained professionally active throughout their medical careers. Many of these men, including Beard, Weir Mitchell, Rockwell, Roberts Bartholow of Philadelphia, Landon Carter Gray of New York City, and Samuel G. Webber of Boston, were associated with the formative years of the ANA, and many served as president of the association at some point during their careers.

The independent neurologists—those who were not members of the ANA—were both younger and more heterogeneous than their "affiliated" brethren who wrote on neurasthenia. Despite the small size of their group—thirty-two authors—it is more difficult to generalize about them than about ANA members. The independent neurologists came from a wider geographical area than did those who joined the ANA, representing equally states of the Northeast and Old Northwest. They, too, tended to reside in urban areas, but their distribution was less predictable and they were more likely to live in "second-tier" cities (250,000–500,000) like Minneapolis, Denver, and Detroit than in the most prestigious medical communities. In fact, 30 percent of these neurologists lived in cities with a population under 100,000, while only 9 percent of the affiliated neurologists were found in such areas.

Most of the independent neurologists in this study were born in the 1860s, and were thus roughly a decade younger than the affiliated group. They were almost as likely to have earned a college de-

gree or at least to have had some college experience prior to entering medical school. They also demonstrated a distinct preference
for top-quality medical schools; the minority in their ranks who
attended lower-rated institutions did so in approximately the same
proportion as did affiliated neurologists. Members of this group
were also likely to have obtained postgraduate experience on the
Continent, particularly in Germany, where neurology was a strong
field. Their pattern of hospital appointments also paralleled that of
the affiliated group; while some served with private and state hospital staffs, far more held appointments at public city institutions.

The most striking difference between the "independents" and
the "affiliateds" was in the apparent inability of the independents
to obtain the prestigious teaching positions that were available to
neurologists who were ANA members. While ANA members taught
almost exclusively at the top medical schools, independents taught
equally at all classes of medical colleges, including such relatively
undistinguished schools as the University of Louisville, the College
of Physicians and Surgeons of Baltimore, and the College of Physicians and Surgeons of Keokuk, Iowa. Given the similarities of
background between the two groups on other matters, it seems
likely that affiliation with the ANA provided additional prestige
and personal contacts that made it possible for ANA members to
secure faculty appointments at more distinguished schools than
those neurologists who were never elected to the national organization. The independent neurologists also belonged to fewer professional societies in general and were less likely to hold office in a
professional organization, another indication that these physicians
were less well connected than their affiliated colleagues. This is not
to say that they were without prestige, but unless they lived in New
York City, Philadelphia, or Chicago where they might belong to a
local neurological society, independent neurologists lacked the
contact with others of their specialty that membership in the ANA
provided.

Typical of the independent neurologists were Henry Waldo Coe,
owner and medical director of a private hospital for nervous and
mental diseases and a prominent citizen of Portland, Oregon; Leo

Melville Crafts, a Harvard graduate who spent his career in Minneapolis; Albert Eugene Sterne, another Harvard alumnus who did postgraduate work in Europe and practiced in Indianapolis; and James G. Kiernan, well known as a defense witness at the Guiteau trial, who began his career in New York City and ended it in Chicago. Other independent neurologists who wrote on neurasthenia included Thomas D. Crothers, a graduate of Albany Medical College, who was long head of Walnut Lodge Hospital in Hartford, Connecticut; Augustus W. Ives of Detroit, who studied for three years abroad before taking his M.D. at the Detroit College of Medicine and Surgery; Thomas C. Ely and William C. Pickett of Philadelphia, graduates of the University of Pennsylvania and Jefferson Medical College respectively; Bernard Oettinger, a graduate of Miami Medical College (Ohio) who practiced in Denver; and Arthur E. Mink, a University of Syracuse alumnus who gained asylum experience in New York before setting up private practice in St. Louis.

It is clear that many of the independent neurologists had excellent academic training and medical experience and were not unlikely to be active members of their profession. While they tended to publish less frequently and to receive less important faculty appointments than their colleagues who were members of the ANA, they were an accomplished group and were frequently leaders in the medical profession at large. It is a chicken-and-egg question whether independent neurologists received less impressive appointments because they often lived in "second tier" cities, or whether they lived in such cities because they could not obtain posts at the top institutions. But it is evident that these neurologists had as much reason to speak with authority on the subject of neurasthenia and nervous disorders as did their colleagues who made up the membership of the American Neurological Association.

Such authority did not devolve as clearly upon the large group of physicians who wrote the greater part of the medical journal literature on neurasthenia, but this fact did not deter them from doing so. These physicians too were well trained and well read, and were evidently eager to treat the diverse complaints of their patients.

The non-neurologists, like their neurological colleagues, showed a distinct preference for the best medical schools. While they attended middle-ranked institutions at a somewhat higher rate than either of the neurological groups and in a few cases even schools ranked academically low, the difference was relatively insignificant. The non-neurologists graduated with greatest frequency in the 1880s and received their licenses in the more restrictive legislative environment of the 1890s. Many non-neurologists also made the trip to Europe to augment their education or, in smaller numbers, remained in the United States and served internships or studied at postgraduate institutions, although this experience was not available for considerably more of them. Most of the non-neurologists who wrote on neurasthenia were probably general practitioners, though few identified themselves as such. The specialists most frequently represented in this group were gynecologists (contributing nineteen articles) and alienists (thirteen articles), oculists (seven articles) and surgeons and electrotherapists, each with six articles.

Alienists, of course, were anxious to expand their terrain, and wanted to prove that they were best qualified to treat neurasthenia because of its close relationship to insanity. The alienists who contributed to the neurasthenic literature were on the whole less distinguished than their neurological counterparts, indicating the neurologists' increasing importance and the alienists' declining prestige. Alienists more frequently attended lower-ranked medical schools, were less likely to study abroad, and usually published less frequently than did neurologists. Nonetheless, the alienists who published on neurasthenia were solid, respectable members of the medical profession. Theodore Willis Fisher of Boston, for example, the eldest of the alienist contributors, received his M.D. from Harvard in 1861. After a tour of duty in the Civil War, he spent most of his career on the staff of various mental institutions in the Boston area and served on the Harvard faculty as a lecturer on mental diseases. Fisher was a stereotypical alienist: he served frequently as an expert witness on mental diseases (he participated in the Guiteau trial, for instance), belonged to the American Medico-Psychological Association, and published on topics of concern to his colleagues like paranoia, monomania, insanity, and cerebral localization.

The alienist group also included George Winslow Foster, a graduate of the Medical School of Maine. Foster, like Fisher, spent most of his career superintending asylums, finishing as superintendent of the new Eastern Maine Insane Asylum in Bangor. Edward Cox Mann, a Long Island College Hospital graduate with Civil War experience, began his career as superintendent of the asylum on Ward's Island in New York City. Like many other alienists, Mann later ran his own asylum, Sunnyside, on the Hudson River near Tarrytown. Similarly, Frank Parsons Norbury of Jacksonville, Illinois, had served in public institutions before founding his own sanitarium, which he directed while serving on the faculty of Illinois College as a lecturer in psycho-physics. Norbury was on the staff of the Pennsylvania Institution for the Education of Feeble-Minded Children and served on the faculty of Keokuk (Iowa) Medical College prior to moving to Illinois in the early 1890s. He also edited *Medical Fortnightly* (St. Louis) and was president of the Mississippi Valley Medical Association and the Illinois Board of Charities. Other alienists who published articles on neurasthenia included Christopher C. Hersman of Pittsburgh, a graduate of the College of Physicians and Surgeons of Baltimore; Hyman M. Folkes of Biloxi, Mississippi, a Tulane graduate; and Floyd S. Crego of Buffalo, an alumnus of the Medical College of Ohio.

Of the non-neurological specialists who wrote on neurasthenia, certainly none was better known than the gynecologist William Goodell. Goodell taught gynecology at Jefferson Medical College from 1870 to 1890 and was a key figure in the founding of both the American Gynecological Society and the American Obstetrical Society, serving as president of both. He was one of the first to warn his colleagues that the radical surgery popular in the late nineteenth century was often unnecessary and to predict a backlash if more caution were not shown. Like the founders of the ANA, Goodell was an elder statesman of his specialty. Robert Latou Dickinson, another gynecologist who contributed to the neurasthenic literature, represented a younger generation of gynecologists whose careers stretched well into the twentieth century. Dickinson was gynecologist and obstetrician to the Brooklyn Hospital and served on the faculty of his alma mater, Long Island Hospital Col-

lege Medical School. He, like Goodell, served as president of the
American Gynecological Society. Dickinson devoted much of his
energy to the American birth control movement and was active in
the National Committee on Maternal Health in the 1920s and
1930s and in the Planned Parenthood Federation from 1939 until
his death in 1950.

Other gynecologists who wrote on neurasthenia ranged from
the influential Howard Atwood Kelly of the Johns Hopkins University faculty to "average" members of the specialty like Willis F.
Hart of Camden, Maine, who was a graduate of the Medical Department of Bowdoin College, and Henry K. Leake, who had graduated from the Kentucky School of Medicine before setting up practice in Dallas, Texas. Like their colleagues in many other specialties,
these physicians were active and well educated. The gynecologists
who wrote on neurasthenia usually did so with one or both of two
purposes: to prove that many neurasthenic symptoms in women
were caused by uterine disturbances and that if "psychical" therapy
were needed in addition to local treatment they could best provide
it. They were already well acquainted with their patients, often attending them regularly in childbirth and for routine gynecological
problems, and felt competent to treat nervous as well as physical
complaints.

Electrotherapists had a natural interest in neurasthenia because
of the reputed effectiveness of electricity in nervous disorders. One
of the most unusual of these was Margaret Abigail Cleaves, a New
York City electrotherapist who received her M.D. from Iowa State
University in 1873. After several professional moves, Cleaves settled
in New York, where she founded and ran the Electro-Therapeutic
Laboratory and Dispensary and served as president of the Woman's
Medical Society. She, like Beard, considered herself to be neurasthenic, and her illness apparently lasted throughout her life.
Much of what is known of her personal life is derived from a book
she published in 1910, *An Autobiography of a Neurasthene. As
Told by One of Them and Recorded by Margaret A. Cleaves*. It
details the life of a woman completely devoted to her career who
struggles constantly against her fears and loneliness to carry on her

work. Other electrotherapists included William Benham Snow, who helped to organize the New York School of Physical Therapeutics; Clara Gary, an 1885 graduate of Boston University School of Medicine who practiced in that city, and Roshier W. Miller, a graduate of the University College of Medicine (Virginia) and resident of Barton Heights, Virginia, near Richmond.

Other contributors to the neurasthenic literature ranged from pathologists and laryngologists to gastroenterologists and occupational therapists. They included the physiotherapist Otto Juettner, the dermatologist/pharmacologist John Veitch Shoemaker, and the hypnotist John Duncan Quackenbos. Besides the unusual and outstanding practitioners, there were many more physicians in cities and towns across the country who wrote on neurasthenia but whose lives remain more obscure to the historian. An idea of their geographical distribution, however, provides some insight into the kinds of services that were available to nervous Americans. Chicago, for example, had the third largest group of contributors to the neurasthenic literature, after New York City and Philadelphia. The city, which grew to a population of 1.7 million in 1900, had a strong contingent of ANA members, including Daniel Brower, Sanger Brown, Archibald Church, James Jewell, Harold Moyer, and Hugh Patrick. Members of the Chicago Neurological Association who were not members of the ANA included Julius Grinker, a graduate of New York University; James Kiernan, who had come to Chicago after practicing for a number of years in New York City, and L. Harrison Mettler, an 1886 graduate of Jefferson Medical College who had taught in Philadelphia before moving to Chicago in 1891. Other Chicago physicians who wrote on neurasthenia included Aria L. Derdiger, a University of Illinois graduate; James Henry Etheridge, a gynecologist and graduate of Rush Medical College; Homer Valmore Halbert, a homeopath; Arthur H. Reading, an eclectic; and Francis Waugh, a graduate of Jefferson Medical College who specialized in materia medica. Both Etheridge and Halbert served on the faculty at their alma maters—Etheridge at Rush and Halbert at Hahnemann Medical College, one of the most respectable of the homeopathic institutions. A walking tour in the early 1900s of the medical offices where nervous Chicagoans could obtain sympathetic, if diverse, care would have found Brown, Moyer, Derdiger, Halbert, and Reading in their offices in the building they shared at 100 State Street in downtown Chicago.

Cincinnati, considerably smaller than Chicago with a population of 325,000 in 1900, nonetheless provided neurasthenic patients with a variety of physicians. It boasted only one neurologist—Philip Zenner, a three-time vice-president of the ANA—but it was also the home of William A. Geohegan, a homeopath; Otto Juettner; Augustus Ravogli, a surgeon; and Charles A. L. Reed. Geohegan was president of the Homeopathic Medical Society of Ohio in 1898; Ravogli served on the state board of medical examiners. Reed was president of the American Association of Obstetricians and Gynecologists in 1898 and president of the AMA in 1901.

Other non-neurological contributors to the neurasthenic literature lived in towns from Bozeman, Montana, to Jackson, Louisiana, and in cities like San Francisco, Detroit, and Boston. Even communities the size of Sioux City, Iowa (population 37,000 in 1900), sometimes supported more than one physician who wrote on nervousness. Fully one-third of all physicians who published on neurasthenia lived in communities under 50,000, and 20 percent lived in towns under 10,000. While there were numerous highly visible figures among the non-neurologists who wrote on neurasthenia, there were many more "average" physicians among them. Thus the group included such men as Joseph M. Aikin of Omaha, Nebraska, a graduate of the University of Iowa; Walter M. Reitzel of Wamego, Kansas, an alumnus of Kansas City Medical College; and G. W. Penn of Humboldt, Tennessee, a graduate of Vanderbilt University School of Medicine. There were a few atypical physicians among them, such as Charles Porter Hart of Wyoming, Ohio, an 1878 graduate of the Chicago Homeopathic Medical College who was an advocate of electrotherapy, and John W. Bowler, a physiotherapist and professional gymnast, who graduated from Dartmouth Medical School and directed the gymnasium there from 1907 to 1936. But most were relatively indistinguishable from their colleagues. As a group they were solid, respectable physicians who were trained at reputable, if not always outstanding, institutions.

The physicians who wrote on neurasthenia had much in common. A few were theorists and pathbreakers, but most were simply conscientious practitioners who were responding to the growing demand of Americans for psychological services. They were, for the most part, motivated by a desire to discover effective means to meet these needs. At issue was which type of practitioner had the most to offer the nervous patient, though this question was usually not addressed directly in the literature. Psychiatric specialists felt that they were best qualified because they limited their practices to mental conditions and thus obtained more experience in treating emotional disorders; other specialists and general practitioners believed themselves to be equally if not more competent due to their knowledge of related physical problems and their ability to treat the whole patient. The resolution of this conflict was to have important implications for twentieth-century patients seeking medical care for emotional problems.

The large group of non-neurological physicians who published most of the journal literature on neurasthenia did so without apology. They felt competent to treat the condition without special training, and most reported success in the handling of their cases. None of these physicians believed that neurasthenic cases should be referred to neurologists; in fact, many of them claimed to have achieved cures after unnamed "famous medical men" had failed. Although the neurasthenic literature contains frequent references to the general failure of the medical profession to understand the disease, the very existence of the body of literature on neurasthenia attests to the fact that there were many physicians throughout the country who sympathized with their nervous patients, and who usually believed they had relieved their suffering or at least had done as good a job as anyone could.

From the patient's point of view, this meant that quality medical care was widely available for psychological problems. It is true that the "best" specialists were located almost exclusively in a few major cities, but their ideas were disseminated to other physicians fairly rapidly. Many of the journal articles in the study were originally presented by rank-and-file physicians as papers at local, state and regional medical meetings; it is evident from the discussions that frequently followed presentations and appeared in published transactions that the views of the authors met a responsive audience and spread well beyond the diverse group of writers to the medical profession in general.

Most physicians, then, were in agreement in their views of nervousness; the differences between them were more social than medical. The greatest diversity is seen in these physicians' relative social positions within the medical community. While a prestigious leadership formulated the most sophisticated medical thought on nervous diseases, their ideas spread rapidly and were adopted by the medical profession at large. The physicians who treated neurasthenia were philosophically aligned but geographically and socially dispersed throughout the country. And contrary to the popular historical view of neurasthenics, the nervous patients described in the medical journal literature were as diverse a group as their physicians. They ranged in age from teenagers to the elderly— though most were young and middle-aged adults—and in social position from bank presidents to shopgirls. The treatment and attribution of cause of nervousness in these patients seems to have depended more on doctors' collective gender and class attitudes than on distinctions based on medical training or specialization.

Predictably, physicians sympathized most with those patients with whom they identified—the middle-class business and professional men most like themselves. Such patients were most likely to be characterized as suffering from overwork and hence described favorably by physicians; fully 69 percent of middle-class men were reported as suffering from overwork and anxiety related to business affairs. While physicians assumed that middle-class men were overworked, they generally ascribed neurasthenia in lower-class males to profligate habits. Only 26 percent of poor males were diagnosed as overworked. Sexual excess was listed as the cause of neurasthenia in 41 percent of these cases, and abuse of alcohol, drugs, or tobacco in 29 percent.

Though physicians' class biases were fairly evident in their deal-
ings with male patients, their views of female neurasthenics were
more complicated. Physicians frequently showed considerable sympathy for poor women, who were not responsible for their positions in life, being dependent on men for their social status. These
women, doctors knew, often had to compete in the workplace—
a man's world for which the weaker sex was unsuited. Overwork
was reported as the cause of nervousness in 26 percent of the
lower-class women studied, but for only 7 percent of middle-class
women. These figures are consistent with the prevalent perception
of "women's work" as being less stressful than men's. But because it
was clear that many middle-class women suffered from neurasthenia, and because physicians accepted a certain amount of nervousness as "natural" in women, physicians were easily persuaded
that neurasthenia in women was caused by feminine biology. Local
disease, excessive childbearing, and assorted "female problems"
were listed as the cause of neurasthenia in 49 percent of middle-
class and 40 percent of poor women.[8]

Although nervousness, as conceived by early neurologists like
Beard and Rockwell, was indeed a disease of the upper classes, this
exclusivity passed rapidly after 1890. By 1900 the diagnosis had
become a convenient catchall for nonspecific complaints. Ironically,
the poor—often treated in public clinics by physicians who had
few diagnostic tools and less time—were by now especially likely
to be pronounced neurasthenic. Some physicians, in fact, began to
charge that the apparent increasing prevalence of neurasthenia was
due to its overuse as a diagnosis among the poor. John K. Mitchell,
the son of Weir Mitchell and also a neurologist, spoke at a meeting
of the Philadelphia County Medical Society in 1905 and held that
"in dispensary reports it [neurasthenia] fills a large place, but I believe this is due to the fact that frequently dispensary patients are
not as carefully examined as private patients."[9] Daniel J. M'Carthy
concurred with Mitchell's opinion in 1908, claiming that "the frequency with which neurasthenia is diagnosed . . . in some outdoor
clinics for nervous diseases is evidence as a rule of a lack of care in
physical and clinical examination."[10] Certainly the poor did not

have access to the new diagnostic tests that were becoming popular by the turn of the century. Urinalysis, blood tests, and examination of the gastric contents were increasingly performed in doctors' offices to rule out physical disorders in patients who complained of fatigue and other mental symptoms.[11] The poor, because they rarely visited private physicians, seldom were offered such tests.

Neurasthenia was thus becoming a diagnosis of last resort for middle-class patients at the same time that its use was increasing among the poor. The democratization of American nervousness occurred not only within the medical community that diagnosed and treated it, then, but also among the patients who suffered from its effects. Though the nervous poor may have received less attention from physicians than middle-class victims, at least the widespread application of the term proved that the lower classes could suffer as much mental pain as the affluent. The recognition of nervous disorders as diseases that transcended both class and gender boundaries was an important step in the transition from Beardianism to Freudianism.

NOTES

1. See Paul Starr, *The Social Transformation of American Medicine* (New York: Basic Books, Inc., 1982), p. 99, for a summary of research estimating irregular strength during the period.

2. Medical school ratings were derived from "Third Classification of Medical Colleges in the United States," *Journal of the American Medical Association,* 60 (1913), 231–34. See Appendix A for more details on the medical school rankings.

3. ANA members were identified almost entirely with major cities. The subprogram crosstabulations isolated the five of the twenty-seven variables dealing with physicians' personal and professional characteristics that were both significant (+/−.05) and had gammas in excess of .30. These variables were date of birth, number of memberships in medical organizations, offices held in medical organizations, faculty positions, and size of residence type. Regression analysis using these five as independent variables and status (the three physician groups) as the dependent variable yielded an $R2$ of .23 with size of residence type accounting for .17, or 74 percent, of the variance between the variables, thus providing statistical confirmation that size of residence type was the most important predictor of status.

4. Barbara Sicherman, "The Uses of a Diagnosis: Doctors, Patients, and Neurasthenia," *Journal of the History of Medicine,* 32 (1977), 44–45.

5. Eric T. Carlson, "George M. Beard and Neurasthenia," in Edward R. Wallace IV and Lucius C. Pressley, eds., *Essays in the History of Psychiatry* (Columbia, S.C.: Wm. S. Hall Psychiatric Institute, 1980), p. 56.

6. Edward C. Spitzka, one of the young turks in the ANA, "characterized Beard as a kind of Barnum of American medicine. The content of his *American Nervousness,* Spitzka added in another review, was 'not worth the ink with which it is printed, much less the paper on which this was done.'" Charles E. Rosenberg, "The Place of George M. Beard in Nineteenth-Century Psychiatry," *Bulletin of the History of Medicine,* 36 (1962), 258. Rosenberg's article remains the best summary of Beard's life and work.

7. Carlson, "George M. Beard and Neurasthenia," p. 54.

8. For more detail on the patient population and physicians' views on class and gender, see F. G. Gosling and J. M. Ray, "The Right to Be Sick: American Physicians and Nervous Patients, 1885–1910," *Journal of Social History,* 20 (1986), 251–67.

9. John K. Mitchell, in discussion following Charles K. Mills, "The Treatment of Neurasthenia," *Proceedings of the Philadelphia County Medical Society,* 26 (1905–6), 393.

10. Daniel J. M'Carthy, "The Neurasthenic Syndrome," *International Clinics,* 18 (1908), 221.

11. For more on these tests and the way in which they were related to changing views of neurasthenia, see F. G. Gosling, "Neurasthenia in Pennsylvania: A Perspective on the Origins of American Psychotherapy, 1870–1910," *Journal of the History of Medicine,* 40 (1985), 188–206.

SIX

Conclusion:
The Modernization of
Nervousness

From the time George Beard introduced the term in 1869 until
the early years of the twentieth century, neurasthenia had ever-
widening applications as physicians adapted the diagnosis to their
own needs. Extending the neurasthenic model, practitioners applied it to all classes and types of patients, from shopgirls to farmers and from the merely tired to the nearly insane. This adapt-
ability accounted for neurasthenia's popularity as the American
disease, but led inevitably to its ultimate demise. As doctors became
more knowledgeable about the characteristics of nervousness they
began to note numerous distinctions of cause and symptom, resulting in cumbersome attempts to classify various emotional disorders as subgroups of the basic illness. The commonalities that
had unified the concept broke down as physicians perceived important dissimilarities among so-called neurasthenics. The American tradition had always placed more emphasis on treatment than
on classification, but the difficulty of achieving permanent cures in
cases of neurasthenia led to dissatisfaction with diagnosis as well
as with therapeutics. European neurologists and psychiatrists had
always paid more attention to definition and theory than their
American counterparts, and after the turn of the century they

made significant changes in the classification of the insanities that attracted their colleagues' attention in the United States.

Three essential factors contributed to the downfall of the neurasthenic model: the increasing emphasis on categorical diagnosis using European criteria, the growing trend toward specialization and scientific medicine that demanded single, specific remedies for specific illnesses, and the triumph of Freud's views of the neuroses and psychoses. Charles Dana, among the best-known authorities on the disease, was one of the first American neurologists to repudiate neurasthenia in favor of new psychological definitions proposed by Kraepelin. In a 1904 article, "The Partial Passing of Neurasthenia," Dana paid tribute to developments in Europe which had already gained credence among leading alienists in the United States: "There have come of late years much clearer ideas of the nature and relationships of the insanities. The analysis of symptoms has been keener and clinical study has been pursued with scientific methods and with an especial enthusiasm. There has been, in fact, a kind of intellectual renaissance in psychiatry which has aroused deeply the interest and respect of neurologists to whom for many years alienism has stood chiefly for politics and stewardship."[1]

Dana ventured that half of all neurasthenics were actually victims of one or more of the "phrenasthenias" (neuroses) or were exhibiting early signs, which Kraepelin termed prodromal, of major psychoses like dementia praecox or manic-depressive insanity. Most of the rest, he believed, were suffering from local conditions like irritable bowel or cardiac disturbance; only a few patients had true nervous exhaustion. Dana anticipated that opposition would arise if America were stripped of its "most distinctive and precious pathological possession," but believed the scientific gains would outweigh any damage done to the national pride by the removal of neurasthenia from "the list of easy diagnoses." In any case, he claimed, those who were deriving the most benefit from the term were "the European professors whom our wandering plutocracy consults; and by whom the diagnosis of the 'American disease' is usually made as the patient is announced."[2]

Though his tone was humorous, Dana's point was worthy of serious consideration. What he proposed was greater attention to precise diagnosis, an idea likely to be rejected by American neurologists more accustomed to treating than to classifying. Dana urged that "the mental state of these patients be carefully examined. The neurologist needs the help of the psychiatrist here, and I hope it will be given. I doubt if neurologists, as a rule, know enough of psychiatrical methods to make always the proper diagnosis of neurasthenia." This remark, coming from a leader of one of the most prestigious American medical specialties, forecast a turning point in the treatment of mental and nervous diseases by American physicians. Increasingly alienists, rechristened psychiatrists, dominated the therapeutics of emotional disturbance, while neurologists turned to the management of nerve diseases and injuries that was their acknowledged domain. General practitioners and nonpsychiatric specialists withdrew from the field as they were no longer able to keep up with psychiatry's expanding body of knowledge. Dana hoped that "this ignorance" among neurologists of psychiatric concepts would be short-lived and that psychiatrists would share their knowledge with their neurological colleagues; then, he believed, "there will develop a readjustment of our neurasthenic states with a knowledge of the psyche as a basis as well as of the *soma*."[3]

The congenial relationship envisioned by Dana was not to be. Psychiatrists, realizing their newly found professional pride and social prestige, were in no hurry to relinquish their gains to longtime rivals, and many neurologists resisted the innovations of new schools of thought. As psychiatric and medical practice in general grew more complex, cross-specialization by nonpsychiatric specialists became more difficult. A few neurologists like James Jackson Putnam and Morton Prince, early converts to Freudian theory, made successful transitions to psychiatric practice, but new members of the psychiatric specialty came from psychological rather than neurological backgrounds. An article written by John E. Donley of Providence, Rhode Island, in 1906 illustrates well the new type of psychologically trained physician. Drawing on the theories of Prince and lesser-known writers, Donley offered a sophisticated discussion of psychological principles that demonstrated the inadequacy of neurasthenia as a diagnostic classification. "To those who have studied neurasthenia in its multiform variations, and have attempted to penetrate beneath the surface of its purely phenomenal manifestations," he wrote, "the inadequacy of present conceptions regarding it must have become apparent."[4]

It was particularly in the attempt to apply abstract models to the living patient that the term fell short, Donley thought. "Having listened to the story of his thousand ills, and having catalogued him in the conventional fashion, we cannot but have experienced the feeling, vague it may be, but none the less real, that somehow we had not gotten to the root of the matter, that there was an intangible something which had eluded us, and which may have been, we suspect, the very essence of the thing we were seeking to fathom."[5] Donley entered into a complicated explanation of personality and asserted that so-called neurasthenia was in simple terms a personality attempting to adapt to an uncomfortable environment. "Any disturbance of these organic [pleasurable] sensations will result in feelings of anxiety, fear, helplessness, and discomfort," he observed.[6] "When . . . tension [balance] is maintained at a normal level we have a stable, healthy person; when for one cause or another this tension becomes lowered we observe its outward expression in a condition of disintegrated, unstable, weakened synthesis, which in our view of it, is in its mildest expression, neurasthenia, and in its more intense grades, hysteria and dissociated or multiple personality."[7]

To prove his point, Donley cited the case of a clergyman currently under his care. This man had suffered a severe nervous breakdown and had ever since exhibited typical signs of neurasthenia: periodic mental and physical exhaustion, obsessions, morbid fears, vasomotor flushing, lack of concentration, depression, and insomnia. In the patient's own words, he felt "like the captain of a steamer who has to keep his eye on everything aboard ship." Donley found an experience of the patient's while dining with a friend "instructive . . . as illustrating the working of an unstable personality in its endeavor to adapt itself to its environment. . . ." On his way to the friend's home, the patient reported, he felt anxious and unsure of his ability to stay through the entire evening. During dinner he felt dizzy and his "fears swooped down upon him with such intensity that it was with difficulty he remained at the table. Recalling to mind, however, what I had told him about neurasthenia being a disintegration of personality . . . he decided to stick it out and to present a solid front to his obsessions, fears, and other sensations." Gradually the fears subsided, "so much so, indeed, that his witticisms evoked a great deal of laughter"; he remained with the group until later in the evening when the conversation turned to subconscious mental activity, reviving his own fears, and he had to hurry away.[8]

The patient had been able to control his mental state temporarily because of the insight given him by therapy. This not only proved that neurasthenias were mental in origin, according to Donley, but also demonstrated that psychic treatment must accompany physical remedies in such cases. "By physical methods," he concluded, "we can give him [the patient] a normal cenesthesis, the physiological basis of personality, but this is not enough. By psychic methods we should teach him properly to evaluate and to assimilate his conscious material, and by so doing to maintain a condition of adaptive stability in relation to his environment."[9]

The psychotherapy Donley described was not that of Freud but of Americans like Prince and Putnam. Though these early psychiatrists admired aspects of Freud's work, their understanding of his theories was incomplete, and their interest lay more in the practical value of his system, i.e., treatment. American interest in psychoanalysis per se did not arise until after Freud's visit to the United States in 1909 and did not constitute a major force in psychiatry until the 1920s. The psychotherapeutic techniques of the early 1900s were extensions of methods long known in American medical practice.[10] Though psychologically oriented physicians were interested in new theories of mental functioning and the implications this understanding could have in practice, their therapeutics were still directed mostly toward suggestion and "education of the patient."

Freud's theories were complex and novel even by European standards. His genius, and his radicalism, lay in his formulation of an integrated system that incorporated and extended elements of psychological principles advanced by other theorists. The philosophers Nietzsche and Schopenhauer contributed to his views of the unconscious, Pierre Janet to his classification of the neuroses and psychoses, and American psychologists like William James and G. Stanley Hall to his theories of child development, dreams, and the maturation of the sexual instinct. His differentiation of the "actual" neuroses from the psychoneuroses illustrates the intricacies of his theories and helps to explain the declining importance of neurasthenia as a diagnostic category. There were three forms of "actual" neuroses, said Freud, so called because they had or once had an organic basis. These were neurasthenia, anxiety neurosis, and hypochondria. Hypochondria developed when an organ somehow attracted attention to itself without the presence of a disease state. Both anxiety neurosis and neurasthenia, the "fatigue neurosis," were sexual in origin. Both resulted from sexual causes such as masturbation, continence, coitus interruptus, or the use of contraceptive devices without "normal" release. Men became weakened by such "unnatural" practices, and women became neurasthenic if thus deprived of the energy they normally acquired through their husbands. Freud believed himself neurasthenic in youth because of the long engagement necessitated by his medical studies and thought that young men in such situations could avoid neurasthenia only by visiting prostitutes. Throughout most of his career Freud held that overwork alone could not cause nervous disorders, although he modified his opinion in 1937.[11]

The psychoneuroses, by contrast, were more clearly of psychological origin. They were caused by conflict and repression, and it was only these disorders—primarily conversion hysteria, obsessions, and phobias—that Freud thought susceptible to psychoanalysis. Though he included the actual neuroses in his general framework of psychological thought and continued to believe in their physical basis, Freud was simply less interested in these disturbances than in those which he found amenable to treatment and for which he developed his psychoanalytic method. In this respect Freud was attuned to the tradition of American medicine. He was primarily concerned with theories that "worked" and was eager to demonstrate the effectiveness of his methodology. This practicality accounted in large part for the acceptance of Freudianism in the United States.

Hale has asserted that psychoanalysis in America differed in significant ways from the variety that flourished in Europe, primarily because of American resistance to the more shocking and pessimistic elements of Freud's theories.[12] This was due partly to the outright rejection of some concepts (particularly those concerning infantile sexuality) by many American physicians, and partly because Freud, in his visit to the United States in 1909, purposely stressed the aspects of his work with most appeal to American audiences. In his lectures at Clark University Freud de-emphasized theory in favor of describing the simplicity and effectiveness of his method of "psychoanalysis."[13] According to Freud, the patient's realization of the incident, real or imagined, that had caused what he termed "conflict and repression" was the essential element that accomplished the cure. American psychiatrists, with their long tradition of "educating" patients, did not fully adopt the Freudian model until after World War I, when substantial numbers of American medical students went to Europe for formal psychoanalytic training. Hence early analysts incorporated into their treatments the elements of Freudianism with which they felt most comfortable and ignored much of the rest. This was consistent with the tradition of psychiatric treatment in America; while practicing physicians were influenced by new theories, they made no dramatic changes in their therapeutic programs. More interested in results than model-building, the medical community had moved increasingly toward mental treatment of psychiatric illnesses since the 1870s, and was as affected by other theories of psychotherapy as by Freud's throughout the first two decades of the twentieth century. Though psychotherapy and even the new morality of the twentieth century has been identified in the public mind with Freudianism, in practice physicians modified and adapted Freud's views of the unconscious and of psychoanalysis just as they had subtly altered Beard's theories of neurasthenia.

Freudian psychoanalysis differed from other psychotherapies in two important respects: its emphasis on sexuality, including the Oedipal complex; and its insistence on self-discovery by the patient. The latter was the major source of Freud's appeal in America and a concept that has had a permanent effect on psychotherapeutic practice. The cathartic or "talking cure" method boldly dropped all necessity for physical remedies and furthermore held out hope for the insane as well as the neurotic. Because of the educational tradition in American psychiatric care and the belief of both patients and physicians in self-determination, the cathartic model was a natural progression in treatment, though the difference in emphasis was significant. As Putnam remarked, other therapists told patients "You can do better if you *try*"; Freud's message was "You can do better if you *know*."[14] The insight gained by dream analysis and recall of early childhood memories, Freud believed, relieved patients of their fears and consequently of their symptoms.

Even this distinctive feature of Freudianism, however, has undergone transition in both theory and practice. To Freud and the early analysts, the ultimate aim of psychoanalysis was the resolution of the Oedipal complex. Later clinicians, following especially the lead of theorists like Karen Horney, have interpreted analysis as a character growth process aimed at reducing the patient's alienation from the real self. In this view patients can "be gradually educated to seek to attain the more constructive goals of analytic therapy."[15] Thus the tradition of patient education, of pointing out errors of thinking and lifestyle, has continued in the treatment of nervous and mental disorders. Those physicians drawn to the field of psychiatry have often been reform-minded; the image of the analyst as a "blank screen" upon whom the patient casts his or her own self-image has not been strictly cultivated in the United States.

Freud's views on sexuality have also been reinterpreted in light of later experience; many psychiatrists and psychologists now see his sexual theories as a phenomenon that reflected conditions in the Victorian era more than the human condition itself. They believe

that the Freudian model was an early and probably inevitable precursor of the sexual revolution that has characterized much of the
twentieth century. While physicians born before 1900 objected to
what they saw as distasteful and unnecessary intrusions into their
patients' sex lives, the public's willingness to be so interrogated was
proved by the popularity of psychoanalysis after 1920. The popu-
lace was ready to cast off the chains of Victorian morality and explore sexuality in all its aspects. Later generations of psychiatrists
found it easier to accept Freud's views of sexuality, but recent evidence suggests that sexual repression has correspondingly become
less important as a cause of mental disturbance in the more per-
missive post–World War I climate.

Psychoanalysis, the treatment that dominated much of twentieth-century psychiatry, has for a number of years been undergoing its own crisis, and for many of the same reasons that led to the
downfall of earlier pathological and therapeutic constructs. After
an initial "honeymoon" period (thought to be a factor in all new
psychiatric therapies), cure rates apparently declined. Historians
have noted that Freud's theories were no more scientific than
Beard's, based solely on a priori reasoning and observation of neu-
rotics without proper controls such as comparisons with populations of normal subjects.[16] Psychoanalysis, more than other forms
of psychiatric treatment, is exclusionary: it requires that patients
be intelligent, articulate, and usually economically successful. Except for small numbers of the institutionalized, it has been available only to private patients. Insurance agencies often provide only
limited coverage for psychiatric care, and the laborious, expensive
psychoanalytic process has discouraged both patients and potential analysts. Freud's emphasis on the mental origins of emotional
disorders discouraged further research on possible organic causes.
His theories could not be proved, except by the effectiveness of the
cure, and there were no means of assessing relative success. Was
less than a 100 percent cure rate acceptable? If so, how much less?
Dissatisfaction with elements of Freudian psychiatry eventually led
to a reevaluation of psychoanalysis itself. Perhaps many mental disorders were, after all, inherited. Certainly some psychiatric ill-

nesses—schizophrenia and mood disorders like depression, for example—seemed to run in families.

In the 1950s the field of biochemical psychiatry began to emerge as a force within the psychiatric profession. This specialty focused on animal research to locate specific mental activities in particular regions of the brain and to explore the role of brain chemistry in mental health and illness. It was discovered that alterations in the production of certain transmitter substances like norepinephrine and dopamine could produce psychotic behavior. In clinical trials drugs like chlorpromazine and haloperidol proved successful in treating schizophrenia, and a group of drugs known as the tricyclic antidepressants were found to produce remission of severe depression in 70 to 80 percent of patients.[17] Lithium produced favorable results in 70 percent of manic patients after only five to ten days of treatment.[18]

But, again, promising avenues of investigation have not solved the problems of nervous and mental disturbance. Drugs do not cure but only control; they must be taken indefinitely and sometimes produce serious and permanent side effects. Psychologists and analytical psychiatrists have protested what they view as an unwarranted eagerness to rely exclusively on drugs when psychotherapy has been shown to be a beneficial adjunct to drug therapy.[19] In some cases return to physical treatment has resulted in the closing of psychiatric hospitals and the "dumping" of ill-prepared patients back into society. And the overemphasis on organic origins of mental disturbance ignores the reality that social and economic conditions contribute to the individual's emotional health.

The management of less acute psychiatric problems, particularly that elusive disorder known as "stress," has also defied scientific solution. Stress, in fact, has become a badge of professional achievement, much like neurasthenia a century ago. Stress is associated with white-collar occupations, high-pressure jobs, and heavy responsibilities; it has even been used to symbolize the professionalization of certain occupations (e.g., "nurse burnout"). Like neurasthenia, stress is a non-life-threatening condition but one that nevertheless produces uncomfortable and disturbing symptoms in its victims—insomnia, depression, loss of ability to concentrate, and eating disorders. It has generated a proliferation of counselors, therapists, and managers with fully as many unusual treatments as nineteenth-century physicians developed for neurasthenia, including exercise therapy, colonic therapy, vitamin therapy, and self-hypnosis, among other methods. Medical specialization has reduced the role of general and family practitioners, gynecologists, and neurologists in treating emotional disturbances, but the continuing need for a varied approach to mental health care has produced new professions—clinical psychology, social work, child development—operating within the medical mainstream to provide counseling services to the anxious Americans of the twentieth century. In addition, faith healers, hypnotists, massage therapists, and practitioners of various persuasions outside of the medical establishment continue to offer treatments for mental ailments as well as physical diseases.

Recently the trend toward specialization in medicine and psychiatry has shown signs of partial reversal. The relatively new specialty of family practice has given added prestige to the "general practitioner" category. Some medical schools and psychiatric residency programs, traditionally limited to one therapeutic persuasion, have attempted to attract faculty with varying backgrounds and viewpoints. And some psychiatrists have even offered advice to physicians wishing to incorporate psychological counseling into their other practice.[20] This form of holistic health care would be preferred by some patients, who could thus obtain counseling without the stigma of visiting a therapist, and would also be satisfying to physicians interested in the psychological dimensions of health care. Such a change, though unlikely to occur on a large scale, would revive the most appealing aspect of nineteenth-century health care—the family physician familiar with the patient's social as well as medical background.

Historical and social experience shows that mental and emotional problems are as timeless as mankind itself, and they remain among the greatest challenges to medical science. If such insights offer no solutions, they at least provide a useful perspective. As we realize that earlier generations have suffered, so too do we learn that earlier medical generations have contributed to our understanding and treatment of such disorders. Most practicing psychiatrists today date modern psychiatry from the beginning of the twentieth century, and many date it from the century's latter half. We should not conclude, however, that the physicians of previous ages were stupid or cruel. As this study suggests, physicians sometimes displayed an understanding of human nature that transcended technology. Barring unforeseen breakthroughs that solve all psychiatric and psychological problems by providing predictable and uniform results, psychiatry will remain a "soft" science admitting of a wide range of practitioners and viewpoints. Consequently the insights of nineteenth-century physicians remain as valid today as they were a century ago.

The literature of neurasthenia challenges the popular view of twentieth-century life as somehow more trying than that of previous eras. Family conflicts, economic problems, and loneliness are inescapable realities of the human condition; probably the idyllic life associated with agrarian society by George Beard's contemporaries and twentieth-century Americans alike has never existed. If anything, existence before the Scientific Revolution may have been more stressful, with family ties broken by earlier deaths and social codes restricting lifestyle options for both men and women. Mental illness, nervous disorders, and stress have doubtless afflicted rich and poor alike throughout history.

NOTES

1. Charles L. Dana, "The Partial Passing of Neurasthenia," *Boston Medical and Surgical Journal*, 150 (1904), 339.
2. Ibid., p. 341.
3. Ibid.
4. John E. Donley, "On Neurasthenia as a Disintegration of Personality," *Journal of Abnormal Psychology*, 1 (1906), 55.
5. Ibid.
6. Ibid., p. 59.
7. Ibid., p. 62.

8. Ibid., p. 65.

9. Ibid., p. 68.

10. The American Psychoanalytic Association was founded in 1911 but had only twenty-three members by 1914, of whom only nine were practicing psychoanalysts. (Nathan G. Hale, Jr., *Freud and the Americans: The Beginnings of Psychoanalysis in the United States, 1876–1917* [New York: Oxford University Press, 1971], p. 325.) This group included young psychiatrists like Freud's translator A. A. Brill, Smith Ely Jelliffe, and William A. White; James Jackson Putnam was the only "elder statesman" in the group. Morton Prince had by this time become disenchanted with Freud, though he continued a psychotherapeutic practice, and many others, like Charles Dana, Charles Mills, Moses Allen Starr, Hugh Patrick, and Frederick Peterson, remained more or less hostile to psychoanalysis.

11. James Strachey, ed. and trans., *The Standard Edition of the Complete Psychological Works of Sigmund Freud*, vol. 1 (London: Hogarth Press, 1966), p. 178.

12. This is a major argument of Hale's *Freud and the Americans*.

13. In his model the patient reclined on a couch in a darkened room with the physician present but unseen. At the first visit the full life history was recounted. Subsequent visits were devoted to exploring elements of this history that the physician found significant, the doctor's participation being to give only enough encouragement to keep the patient talking.

14. James Jackson Putnam, "On the Etiology and Treatment of the Psychoneuroses" (1910), in *Addresses on Psychoanalysis* (London: International Psycho-Analytical Press, 1921), p. 66.

15. Benjamin J. Becker, "Whither Psychoanalysis," *American Journal of Psychoanalysis*, 40 (1980), 291.

16. M. B. Macmillan, "Beard's Concept of Neurasthenia and Freud's Concept of the Actual Neuroses," *Journal of the History of the Behavioral Sciences*, 12 (1976), 389.

17. David S. Segal et al., *Foundations of Biochemical Psychiatry* (Boston: Butterworths, 1976), p. 139.

18. Ibid., p. 140.

19. Ibid., p. 12.

20. An example of this literature is Charles L. Bowden and Alvin G. Burstein, *Psychosocial Basis of Health Care*, 3d ed. (Baltimore: Williams & Wilkins, 1983), especially chap. 18, pp. 281–90.

S. Weir Mitchell examining a Civil War veteran at the clinic of the Orthopaedic Hospital in Philadelphia. From Anna Robeson Burr, *Weir Mitchell: His Life and Letters* (New York: Duffield, 1929).

A corner in the Battle Creek Sanitarium laboratory of experimental hydrotherapy. From Kellogg, *Rational Hydrotherapy.*

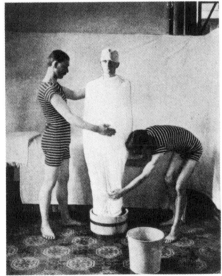

The wet sheet rub: applying the sheet (second step). From John Harvey Kellogg, *Rational Hydrotherapy: A Manual of the Physiological and Therapeutic Effects of Hydriatic Procedures, and the Technique of Their Application in the Treatment of Disease* (Philadelphia: Davis, 1901).

Compressed air chamber developed by J. Leonard Corning. From *Medical Record*, 40 (1891).

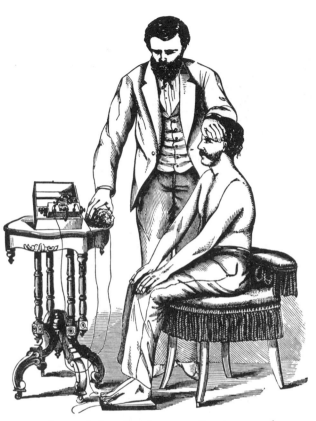

General faradization: application to the head. From George Miller Beard and A. D. Rockwell, *A Practical Treatise on the Medical and Surgical Uses of Electricity*, 5th ed. rev. (New York: Wood, 1881).

Central galvanization, second stage. From Beard and Rockwell, *Practical Treatise on Uses of Electricity*.

Franklinization. From Beard and Rockwell, *Practical Treatise on Uses of Electricity.*

Maplewood Sanitarium. From *Polk's Medical Register* (Detroit: R. L. Polk, 1906).

THE "RETREAT" is a large, quiet home, for nervous and morbid mental cases, comprising a brick residence and three frame cottages, in a beautiful park, containing forty acres of natural timber. The treatment consists in rest, baths, massage, electricity, medicine, outdoor life and suitable trained nurses for companions. Address

DR. GERSHOM H. HILL or DR. J. C. DOOLITTLE, Des Moines, Iowa.

The Retreat. From *Polk's Medical Register.*

The White Sanitarium

DALLAS, TEXAS

For the Treatment of Chronic Alcoholism, Tobacco and Drug Addictions.
Also Neurasthenia or Nerve Exhaustion.

No fixed formulæ. All cases are examined and treated scientifically on their individual merits.

We will accept any case and perfect a cure before requiring one cent of pay, only demanding satisfactory evidence of ability to pay the fee when cure is perfected.

Free literature supplied on application.

S. J. WHITE, M. D., Physician in Charge.   **W. F. WHITE, Business Manager.**

The White Sanitarium. From *Polk's Medical Register.*

Kenilworth Sanitarium
KENILWORTH, ILLINOIS.
Telephones: Kenilworth 78; Evanston 778.

The Kenilworth Sanitarium is entirely new and was constructed and equipped to supply the demand for a first-class neuropathic and psychopathic hospital, easily accessible to the residents of Chicago and vicinity.

It is situated about half a mile due west of the Kenilworth station [C. & N. W. Ry.,] six miles north of Chicago, from which, in addition to steam and trolley cars, it may be reached at all seasons of the year by good carriage road.

The grounds consist of ten acres lying nearly one and one-half miles from the shore of Lake Michigan and the distance from car lines and other sources of noise is such as to insure practically complete rural quietude.

The accommodations for patients consist of six independent groups of from six to seven large bedrooms, some of which are so constructed as to be impervious to noise, a spacious sitting-room and corridor and two bath-rooms, one of which in each group is planned to be used en suite when desired. There are also four separate dining-rooms. Thus it will be seen that the supreme importance of thorough classification in institutional treatment of the neuroses has been duly recognized.

There is an electric passenger elevator, electric lighting, and a complete system of telephones.

The warming is by steam, both direct and indirect radiation having been provided to each sleeping and sitting room.

An abundance of pure water is supplied from a bored well, 148 feet deep, on the premises.

There are twelve bath-rooms for the use of patients, six of which may be used en suite. They all have the most modern open plumbing, ceramic tile floors, and porcelain and enameled fixtures. Both floors and finish are of hardwood throughout the building, and the appointments are all first class.

Ample provisions have been made for the employment of the most approved diagnostic and therapeutic methods, it being rather the purpose of the management to actively ameliorate suffering and promote recovery than merely to extend custodial care to those who are unable to live at large. In other words, it is aimed to conduct a neuropathic and psychopathic hospital rather than a mere asylum.

DR. SANGER BROWN, Physician in Charge

Telephone Central 3707.   Chicago Office, 100 State Street.

Kenilworth Sanitarium. From *Polk's Medical Register*.

Francis Xavier Dercum. From Derek Denny-Brown, ed., *Centennial Anniversary Volume of the American Neurological Association* (New York: Springer Publishing Co., 1975). Reprinted by permission.

William Alexander Hammond. From Fielding Hudson Garrison, *History of Neurology*, rev. ed. by Lawrence C. McHenry, Jr. (Springfield, Ill.: Thomas, 1969). Courtesy of Charles C. Thomas, Publisher.

Edward Constant Seguin. From Garrison, *History of Neurology*.

Frank Parsons Norbury. From Watson, *Physicians and Surgeons of America*.

John Duncan Quackenbos. From Irving Allison Watson, *Physicians and Surgeons of America: A Collection of Biographical Sketches of the Regular Medical Profession* (Concord: Republican Press Association, 1896).

George Miller Beard. From *New England Journal of Medicine,* 219 (1938). Reprinted by permission.

Henry Waldo Coe. From Watson, *Physicians and Surgeons of America.*

John Veitch Shoemaker. From Watson, *Physicians and Surgeons of America.*

Theodore Willis Fisher. From Watson,
Physicians and Surgeons of America.

James Stewart Jewell. From Denny-
Brown, *Centennial Anniversary Vol-
ume of the American Neurological
Association.*

Charles Loomis Dana. From *Journal
of Nervous and Mental Disease,* 83
(1936).

APPENDIX A

Sources and Method

To date, historians have focused relatively little attention on neur-asthenia. Most of the work that has been done has been based on the writings of George Beard and other leading neurologists of the period.[1] While this scholarship has the virtue of detailing the views of elite physicians, it does not measure the extent to which "ner-vousness" proved useful to the medical community at large, nor does it shed light on the process by which elite physicians' ideas about neurasthenia were transmitted through the medical ranks. Furthermore, much remains to be done to relate concerns of the "new social history" to the history of medicine—questions about the gender and class attitudes of physicians, for example, and about physician specialization and status.

This study attempts to bring social history and medical history closer together by applying some of the statistical techniques that have been widely used by various social and political historians. These techniques, confined primarily in this study to crosstabula-tions, are not at all complex and can be easily learned and applied by historians with relatively little exposure to statistics or quan-titative training. While the methods employed and described here will doubtless seem pedestrian to many social scientists, their value to medical history is considerable simply because they have been so little used in the field thus far. Crosstabulations provide both "tests of significance," which indicate whether the relationship between variables is reliable, and "gamma," which measures the strength of the relationship, making it possible to decide which relationships have the most explanatory power. Much of the analysis in the present study involved measuring the relationships between physicians, a host of variables pertaining to their views on neurasthenia, and to differences between patients. Controlling for time, based on year of publication, made it possible to discover when changes in physicians' perceptions of neurasthenia took place. The research design thus measured changes in beliefs about and management of neurasthenia from its "discovery" to its displacement by the dynamic models of twentieth-century psychiatry.

Virtually all of the medical journal literature on neurasthenia published between 1870 and 1910 was analyzed for the study. This period represents the years between Beard's earliest publications on neurasthenia and the deterioration of the neurasthenic model because of the increasing interest by the 1910s in the ideas of Sigmund Freud. A list of articles was compiled from *Index Medicus*, Series I, volumes 1–21 (1879–99), and Series II, volumes 1–8 (1903–10), and the *Index Catalog of the Library of the Surgeon-General's Office, United States Army,* Second Series, volume 11 (1906), and Third Series, volume 9 (1929). Some articles with neurasthenia in the title were excluded because they did not actually discuss the disease, while some general articles on nervous diseases were included because they contained significant sections on neurasthenia. Since a major aim of the study was to trace the transmission of ideas about neurasthenia, monographic literature, written primarily by leaders in the field to formalize and extend theories usually stated more concisely in article form, were excluded from the study. Articles in popular magazines, containing public positions taken by doctors and lay writers alike, were also excluded. The resulting 332 articles represent virtually the entirety of the medical journal literature on neurasthenia, excluding reprints and abstracts. They were written by 262 American physicians who offered their individual interpretations of the diseases—its causes, symptoms, most likely victims, and preferred treatments. Eighty-nine of these physicians also reported on individual patients, which provided a study population of 307 "nervous" men and women.[2]

To analyze this mass of data it was necessary to systematize the information. Data derived from patient case records, from content analysis of the medical journal literature, and from biographical sources relating to the physicians who wrote on neurasthenia, was rendered into machine-readable form. A three-part code was devised to record information about patient cases (Chapter 2), about physicians' beliefs concerning the causes, symptoms, and treatment of neurasthenia (Chapters 3 and 4), and personal and professional information about the physicians themselves (Chapter 5). Case records are extremely valuable as social history because they provide important information about otherwise forgotten men and women and because they reveal the recording physician's attitudes about the patient and the disease in question. Among data often reported were age, sex, occupation, and marital status, as well as the symptoms and causes of neurasthenia in the individual case, and treatment method employed. In many instances, the length, severity, and previous handling of the case, and sometimes the success of treatment and the values or personal qualities of the patient, were also discussed. Thus, the 307 patient cases reported in the journal literature provide collective evidence of who neurasthenics were and how they coped with the problems that beset them. Data were also collected on the extent to which authors agreed with Beard's premises, where the paper was read or published, the authorities cited, and the content of discussions that took place following presentations at medical meetings.

Information was recorded in as raw a form as possible. For example, physicians' medical schools were recorded as given and later placed in one of three classifications reflective of the institution's quality.[3] Content analysis variables, such as those attempting to measure patients' personal values or the extent to which physicians agreed with Beard's views of neurasthenia, were coded by recording the exact language used by physicians. In many cases resulting value lists were so lengthy that statistical analysis could not be performed until variables were recoded or "collapsed" into a smaller number of categories. This process involved a number of judgment calls as values were placed on a continuum and then grouped according to similarity. Terms used to describe patient heredity, for instance—"hardy stock," "tainted," "neuropathic," etc.—were eventually placed in categories of good, fair, and poor.

The analysis of physicians relied on information gathered from a variety of medical directories. These publications included information on medical training, professional memberships and specialty affiliations, publication records, hospital and clinic experience, faculty appointments, and other personal and professional characteristics. The directories devoted exclusively to the medical profession fall into two categories—those that listed virtually all physicians but provided only limited information on each, and those that included detailed biographical sketches of leading physicians. In the former category are the *American Medical Directory: A Register of Legally Qualified Physicians of the United States and Canada* (Chicago: American Medical Association Press, 1906), and *Polk's Medical Register and Directory of North America*, 10th ed. rev. (Detroit: R. L. Polk & Co., Publishers, 1908), the *AMD* being the more valuable. *Polk's* provided information on sectarian affiliation, medical school, and year of graduation, and sometimes office location and licensing status. Occasional lengthier entries included institutional affiliations and organizational memberships. The *AMD* provided uniform information on individual physicians, including year of birth, medical school and year of graduation, year of license, sectarian affiliation, memberships in national, state, and local societies, and, occasionally, office address and office hours. Two hundred and thirty-three of the 262 doctors in the study (89 percent) were listed in either the *AMD* or *Polk's*. While this is not a statistically valid cross section of all doctors, the high percentage of "hits" suggests the possibility of studying other physician groups quantitatively; there are few other nineteenth-century populations for whom so much analyzable data is available.

The other category of medical directories included lengthy and usually laudatory accounts of prominent physicians. Among these publications were Howard A. Kelly, ed., *Cyclopedia of American Medical Biography* (Philadelphia: W. B. Saunders, 1912), Kelly and Walter L. Burrage, eds., *Dictionary of American Medical Biography: Lives of Eminent Physicians of the United States and Canada, From the Earliest Times* (New York: Appleton, 1928), John Shrady, ed., *Cyclopedia of American Physicians and Surgeons* (New York: Hershey Publishing, 1903), R. French Stone, ed., *Biography of Eminent American Physicians and Surgeons* (Indianapolis: Carlon & Hollenbeck, 1894), and Irving A. Watson, ed., *Physicians and Surgeons of America: A Collection of Biographical Sketches of the Regular Medical Profession* (Concord: Republican Press Association, 1896). All of these "farmed out" the sketches to collaborators, some of whom, inevitably, were more careful than others. These guides provide relatively valuable information on all of the variables pertinent to the doctor code; their major limitation was that they contained only about 30 percent of the physicians in the study (although even this percentage indicates the relatively high status of this physician population). While excessively florid, the sketches do yield information on publications, medical school professorships, postgraduate training, medical and nonmedical memberships and offices held, and, occasionally, religious and political affiliations. While it was not the focus of this study, they also provided a sense of career pattern unavailable in either the *AMD* or *Polk's;* but dates given in the sketches should be treated cautiously and, if possible, compared with those in other guides.

Another source, Derek Denny-Brown, ed., *Centennial Anniversary Volume of the American Neurological Association, 1875–1975* (New York: Springer Publishing Company, 1975), was unusual in being published recently as a commemorative volume. It proved particularly useful because it contained sketches of ANA presidents and an accurate roster of all past ANA members. The dates in Denny-Brown were highly reliable and provided a useful check on those ANA members who also appeared in one or more of the biographical directories. Additional information on elite physicians was gleaned from *Who Was Who in America, Historical Volume, 1607–1896: A Component Volume of Who's Who in*

American History (Chicago: Marquis, 1963), and *Who Was Who: A Companion to "Who's Who," Containing the Biographies of Those Who Died during the Period 1897–1950*, volumes 1–3 (Chicago: Marquis, 1963). These entries were brief and highly reliable and were used as authorities in cases of discrepancies between sources.

Though this application of statistical analysis is modest compared with efforts in other fields of history, it does demonstrate that quantitative techniques can be effectively employed in the history of medicine. Biographical data on physicians, content analysis of the medical literature, and case records of individual patients all provide a wealth of information that lends itself to systematic analysis. It is hoped that other medical historians will undertake similar quantitative research projects in order to enhance our understanding of physicians and of their relationships with patients.

NOTES

1. Among those who have published work dealing either directly or incidentally with neurasthenia and Beard and their place in the history of American neurology and psychiatry are Bonnie Ellen Blustein, "New York Neurologists and the Specialization of American Medicine," *Bulletin of the History of Medicine*, 53 (1979), 170–83; Anita Clair Fellman and Michael Fellman, *Making Sense of Self: Medical Advice Literature in Late Nineteenth-Century America* (Philadelphia: University of Pennsylvania Press, 1981); Sy P. Fullinwider, "Neurasthenia: The Genteel Caste's Journey Inward," *Rocky Mountain Social Science Journal*, 2 (1974), 1–9; James B. Gilbert, *Work without Salvation: America's Intellectuals and Industrial Alienation, 1880–1910* (Baltimore: The Johns Hopkins University Press, 1977), pp. 31–43; Nathan G. Hale, Jr., *Freud and the Americans: The Beginnings of Psychoanalysis in the United States, 1876–1917* (New York: Oxford University Press, 1971); John S. Haller and Robin M. Haller, *The Physician and Sexuality in Victorian America* (Urbana: University of Illinois Press, 1974), pp. 5–43; Charles E. Rosenberg, "The Place of George M. Beard in Nineteenth-Century Psychiatry," *Bulletin of the History of Medicine*, 36 (1962), 245–59; Barbara Sicherman, "The Paradox of Prudence: Mental Health in the Gilded Age," *Journal of American History*, 62 (1976), 890–912; Sicherman, "The Uses of a Diagnosis: Doctors, Patients, and Neurasthenia," *Journal of the History of*

Medicine, 32 (1977), 33—54; Sicherman, *The Quest for Mental Health in America, 1880—1917* (New York: Arno Press, 1980); and M. D. Macmillan, "Beard's Concept of Neurasthenia and Freud's Concept of the Actual Neuroses," *Journal of the History of the Behavioral Sciences,* 12 (1976), 376—90. Older but still useful are Philip P. Wiener, "G. M. Beard and Freud on 'American Nervousness,'" *Journal of the History of Ideas,* 17 (1956), 269—74, and Henry Alden Bunker, "From Beard to Freud: A Brief History of the Concept of Neurasthenia," *Medical Review of Reviews,* 36 (1930), 109—14.

2. There were more than 307 neurasthenics reported in the literature, but many writers based their comments on their collective experiences and did not discuss individual cases, or did not provide enough information about individual patients to make coding possible.

3. Ratings were obtained from "Third Classification of Medical Colleges of the United States," *Journal of the American Medical Association,* 60 (1913), 231—34. This report of the AMA's Council on Medical Education gathered information on twenty-seven items relevant to institutional curricula and arrived at a final ranking by awarding schools points in ten categories. The AMA report placed schools in four categories: Class A plus, "acceptable medical colleges"; Class A, "colleges lacking in certain respects but otherwise acceptable"; Class B, "colleges needing general improvements to be made acceptable"; and Class C, "colleges requiring a complete reorganization to make them acceptable." Because the AMA report classified so many schools as Class A plus and Class A, and because the physicians who wrote on neurasthenia attended high-rated institutions most frequently, Class B and C schools were combined for the purposes of this study into Category C; Class A plus is referred to as Class A, and Class A as Class B in order to make delineations more distinct.

Patient Occupations

Professional (N=79)

Banker
Broker
Businessman; position of
  responsibility
Civil engineer
Clergyman
College faculty
Contractor
Gentleman; well off
Hospital superintendent
Lawyer
Manufacturer
Merchant
Newspaper editor
Physician
Politician

Skilled/Semiskilled (N=56)

Accountant/bookkeeper
Animal trainer
Bank teller
Bartender
Bill collector
Brass polisher
Butcher

Carpenter
Cigar maker
Clerk
County officer
Designer
Druggist
Engraver
Farmer
Fisherman
Furrier
Gambler
Hotelkeeper
Instructress/bookkeeper; sewing
  machine establishment
Machinist
Mechanic
Mechanical draftsman
Nurse
Oyster opener/dealer
Painter
Railroad engineer
Realtor
Salesperson
Schoolteacher
Seamstress
Storekeeper
Tailor

Telegraph copyist
Timekeeper; brass factory
Traveling salesman
Wire weaver

Housewives (N=44)

Laborers (N=21)

Car cleaner
Housekeeper
Laborer; unspecified
Print shop laborer

Railroad laborer
Servant
Stevedore
Waiter
Waitress

Other (N=17)

Asylum inmate
Dependent
Retired
Student

Index